Magic Mind Secrets for Building Great Riches Fast

Tyler G. Hicks

Parker Publishing Company
West Nyack, New York

LIBRARY OF CONGRESS
CATALOG CARD NUMBER: 76-159275

PRINTED IN THE UNITED STATES OF AMERICA
ISBN—0-13-543934-5
B&P

What This Book
Does for You

E$_{}$very man and woman who builds great wealth uses *magic mind secrets* of some kind to put his fortune together. These magic mind secrets are universal—anyone, including *you*, can use them! And they are so *powerful* that everyone who uses the magic mind secrets given in this book is almost certain to build great wealth quickly and surely.

Why fumble trying to find the secret combination that opens the door to *instant* riches when the secrets are here, in this book, ready to use?

My four other wealth and riches books (which are listed at the front of *this* book) were immediate best sellers. People from all over the world bought, and still buy, and use these books.

In my thousands of discussions with beginning wealth-builders throughout the world, one fact keeps repeating itself to me. This fact is:

> Most beginners are ready to build a great fortune except for one item: They don't recognize that magic mind secrets are as important as any other element—money, ideas, ambition, and so on—in building great riches *fast*.

And why are these magic mind secrets so important? Because, good reader and fellow wealth-builder, the greatest fortunes begin as an idea in someone's mind. One good idea, properly manipulated by a wealth-builder's mind, can grow into a world-wide fortune.

Scientists say that *your* brain contains three billion cells and more circuits connecting these cells than *all* the telephone wires in *all* of North America! Is it any wonder then that when you apply *your* mind to building enormous riches that the results are truly magical? Yes, you have within *you* all the skills you need to be the richest man or woman in the world. And when I say this I mean rich in money, rich in happiness, rich in friends, and rich in love for others!

So come with me, good reader, and soon-to-be-successful fortune builder, and watch and listen while I show you how to:

- Have enormous confidence in yourself
- Use your mind to plot your way to riches
- Build your health while building your wealth
- Follow your stars to a great fortune
- Exert a rich mental attitude in everything you do
- Make your ambitions pay off in *big money*
- Use other people's money to make money for *you*
- Find goodness everywhere you go
- Analyze your personal wealth-building skills
- Apply science to your wealth-building efforts
- Figure your best wealth-building days
- Put psychic power to work in your daily money life
- Use psycho-cybernetics to control your wealth
- Apply the newest concepts to attract riches

Yes, fellow fortune-builder, *you* are on the brink of enormous wealth—if you tag along with me. I have nothing to sell you, *except your success!* Hundreds and hundreds of beginning fortune-builders who try my methods report *instant* success. Their income grows each year and a number become millionaires within three years after putting my ideas to work in their wealth efforts.

To make this book doubly valuable and helpful to you, I've listed hundreds of other books and sources of information that helped put me in the millionaire's league. Read as many of these books as you can and you'll enormously improve your chances for great success.

Remember—nothing succeeds like success—*your success!* So let's start now to make you wealthy, healthy, and wise. Don't waste another moment—turn the page to your river of pure gold which starts with the first page of chapter one. And good luck!

Tyler G. Hicks

Contents

Chapter two—continued

*in Your ESP . . . . Get More from Your Thought Power
. . . . Long-Distance Mind Power Will Work for You Too
. . . . Six Rules for Seeing Thought Pictures . . . . Multiply
Your Mind-Magic . . . . Mind-Magic Can Make You Rich
. . . . Quadruple Your Income Using Mind-Magic . . . .
Set Your Second Mind to Work . . . . Create Mental Pic-
tures of Your Wealth . . . . Why Mental Pictures Pay Off.*

*Why Health and Wealth Rhyme . . . . Stopping Work
Can Damage Your Health . . . . Try My Magic Health
Formula . . . . Combine Health and Wealth . . . . Turn
Your Pains into Gains . . . . Draw Your Health Profile
. . . . Make Health Your Wealth Goal . . . . From Wheel-
chair to Riches in a Year . . . . Take Action Fast to
Acquire Health with Wealth . . . . Listen to Your Doctor
But Make Money! . . . . Build Riches Anywhere . . . . Put
Your Know-how to Work . . . . Become Your Own Money
Source . . . . Aim at Capital-Gain Profits . . . . Be a Big
Winner in the Health-Wealth Game . . . . Take Off Now
for Better Health, Greater Wealth.*

*Use the Stars to Guide Your Fortune Hunting . . . . What
Astrology Does for People . . . . What Astrology Is . . . .
Why Astrology May Help You . . . . Analyze Business
Associates with Astrology . . . . Surround Yourself with
Money . . . . Sell—Borrow—Buy—Repay—Profit . . . .
Collect from Your Sellers . . . . Put Your Horoscope to
Work . . . . Make Astrology Work for You . . . . Con-
sider Becoming an Astrologer . . . . Combine Astrology
with Self-Confidence . . . . Get Rich Fast Using Your
Horoscope . . . . Seek, and Do, the Unusual . . . . Be Sure*

Chapter four—continued

of Your Facts . . . . Test Your Ideas . . . . Work Other Combinations.

Control Your Thoughts . . . . What Is a Rich Mental Attitude? . . . . What an RMA Does for You . . . . Turn Your RMA into Big Money . . . . Get Rich in Less Than One Year . . . . Think Rich and Be Rich . . . . Seek the Simple, Big Money Business . . . . Develop Your New Way of Life Using RMA . . . . Put Other People's Money to Work for You . . . . Dream Yourself to Riches . . . . Feel Good—Help Others . . . . Back an Idea Using Your RMA . . . . Go the Public Route with RMA . . . . How the Public Can Help You . . . . You Can't Miss with a Strong RMA . . . . For Positive Results, Hook Speed to RMA.

Convert Ambitions to Actions . . . . Why Your Actions Are Important . . . . Know How Your Mind Works . . . . Put Self-Motivation into Your Wealth Search . . . . Understand Self-Motivation Unlimited . . . . Seven Questions to Tell You as It is . . . . Five Wealth-Builders Who Hit Big Money . . . . Never Neglect Auto-Hypnosis in Your Wealth Search.

Borrowing Money Is Fun and Profitable! . . . . Advantages of Borrowing OPM . . . . Know Your Sources of OPM . . . . Tap Your Bank for a Personal Loan . . . . Try a Business Loan from Your Bank . . . . Eight Sure-Fire Mind Secrets to Loan Success . . . . Put a Finance Company to Work

Chapter seven—continued

*for You . . . . Can a Professional Money Lender Help Me?
. . . . Insurance Companies Are Loaded with OPM . . . .
See a Financial Broker for the Money You Need . . . .
How to "Beat the System"—Honestly . . . . Venture-
Capital Firms Have Bundles of OPM . . . . Try a State
Business Loan . . . . Is the SBA Your Source of OPM?
. . . . Sell Your Company Stock to the Public . . . . Private
Stock Offerings Can Help Too . . . . OPM Is Your Fast
Way to Wealth.*

*Find Money Wherever You Go! . . . . Get Ready for In-
stant Riches . . . . Decide What You Want . . . . Three
Who Decided What They Wanted . . . . Attract Good
Luck to Yourself . . . . Pyramid Serendipity to Riches
. . . . Catch the Good Things in Life . . . . Turn Your
Dreams into Money . . . . Build Your Income Fast . . . .
Take Action Today for Results Tomorrow.*

*Tap an Infinite Source of Zest . . . . Analyze People
Quickly and Easily . . . . From Rags to Riches in a Year
. . . . Learn the Truth About Business Deals . . . .
Combine Your Zest and Brain Power . . . . Use Other
Character Analysis Techniques . . . . Start Now to Use
Handwriting Analysis . . . . Apply Body Language Signals
. . . . Three Who Made It Big . . . . Mail-Order Way to
Wealth . . . . Pick Your Money Path and Run! . . . . Get
Started—Don't Waste Time . . . . Build Fast from Small
Beginnings . . . . Pyramid Your Way to Wealth . . . . Put
Your Plans into Action . . . . Take the Real-Estate Route
to Wealth . . . . Go First Class—All the Way . . . . Get
the Facts You Need . . . . Plan Your Moves Carefully
. . . . Buy Low—Sell High . . . . Use Your Go-Power Now.*

Chapter ten—How to Build Easy-Money Riches Using Science 155

Put Science to Work for Yourself Today . . . . Use Statistics to Build Wealth . . . . Put Your Statistics to Work . . . . See How Others Do It . . . . Be a Numbers Businessman . . . . Don't Let Averages Fool You . . . . Build Your Fortune in the Unusual . . . . Money Averages Pay Off . . . . Wheel and Deal Your Way to Wealth . . . . How Wheeler-Dealers Work . . . . Work the Way Wheeler-Dealers Do . . . . Know the Ins and Outs of Interest . . . . Put OPM to Work for Yourself . . . . Use Random Samples to Get Fast Data . . . . Make a Million by Investing Only Your Time . . . . Plan Your Way to Wealth . . . . How Plans Pay Off . . . . Budget Your Way to Great Wealth . . . . Keep Budgets Simple . . . . Make Science Pay Off for You.

Chapter eleven—How to Figure Your Best Money-Making Days 173

Work Your Mind and Body . . . . Three Who Hit It Big . . . . Find Your Best Days . . . . Keep a Record of Your Moods . . . . Moods Can Pay Off . . . . Make Your Moods Your Money-Magic . . . . Try Biorhythm in Your Wealth Search . . . . Plot Your Biorhythm . . . . Have Your Friends Help You . . . . Move Ahead to Great Wealth . . . . Make Instant Cash Yours by Mail . . . . Never Neglect Your Moods.

Chapter twelve—Putting Psychic Power to Work in Your Money Life 187

Understand Psychic Money Power . . . . Develop Your Psychic Money Powers . . . . Three Who Mastered Psychic Money Powers . . . . See Your Future Riches . . . . Corner a Profitable Idea . . . . Get with the Money . . . . Borrow Your Way to a Great Fortune . . . . Practice, Practice, Practice . . . . Know the Power of Psychic Forces . . . . Seek the Magic in Psychic Money Powers . . . . Psychic

Chapter twelve—continued

*Money Power Works Everywhere . . . . Pick Your Product
Using Psychic Powers . . . . Earn Money from the Entire
World . . . . Put Your Psychic Money Powers to Work
. . . . Psychic Money Power Really Pays Off.*

**Chapter thirteen—Using Psycho-Cybernetics
to Control Your Wealth** **203**

*Know the Basics of Psycho-Cybernetics . . . . Think Big—
Win Big . . . . Plan Your Way to Riches . . . . Use the
Psycho-Cybernetics Way to Wealth . . . . Develop a Posi-
tive Self-Image . . . . Become an Instant Millionaire . . . .
Get All the Facts . . . . Keep Setting Goals for Yourself
. . . . A Big-Money Goal and Your Self-Image . . . . Seek
the Unusual Everywhere . . . . Turn Your Self-Image into
Cash . . . . Switch a Good Idea into Millions . . . . Sell
for More Than You Pay . . . . Learn from Everyone . . . .
You Must Like Yourself.*

**Chapter fourteen—How to Grow Richer with
the Newest Mind Methods** **217**

*Think the Big-Success Way . . . . Try the Newest Ap-
proaches . . . . Brainstorm Your Way to Wealth . . . .
Hold Private Brainstorming Sessions . . . . Good Ideas
Make Money . . . . Never Stop Trying . . . . Try the Hori-
zontal Think . . . . Put Your Brain to Work . . . . Build
on Your Skills . . . . Maybe You Need Group Think . . . .
Cure Problems Before They Occur . . . . Make Dry Runs
. . . . Practice Now—Profit Sooner . . . . Put Logic to Work
for Yourself . . . . Watch Logic at Work . . . . Increase
Your Creativity . . . . Creativity Really Pays Off . . . .
Make All Your Ideas Good Ones . . . . Weed Out the Bad
Ideas . . . . Try Synthesis to Improve Your Ideas . . . .
Recognize Every Man's Worth . . . . Build Your Riches
Fast.*

one

How to Get Rich by Building Your Self-Confidence

The most powerful tool any man can have for building great riches fast is his self-confidence. Why? Because with the right amount of self-confidence you can overcome any other disadvantages you may have.

Self-confidence is the concentrated fuel that helps you:

• Get around the largest obstacles
• Find paths through unknown worlds
• Do what you never thought possible
• Build riches quickly and surely

Let's see how you can put the magic powers of self-confidence to work in your life—starting this instant.

Know What Self-Confidence Is

Self-confidence is a firm belief in your abilities, ideas, and goals which motivates you to take action to achieve your objectives in life. When you have adequate self-confidence you:

- Keep trying even when the going gets rough
- Push your ideas ahead until they become reality
- Achieve the goals you set for yourself
- Never accept failure in any important work
- Refuse to accept excuses for poor performance

You're self-confident when you lead a *directed* life which *you've* chosen. You are master of your fate—captain of your soul. Self-confidence gives your life and work meaning and importance. Further, self-confidence improves your ability to cope with all kinds of social situations.

Check Your Self-Confidence Rating

Here's a handy checklist to help you find how much self-confidence you have. Fill it out now to discover if a lack of self-confidence is keeping you from being rich.

MY SELF-CONFIDENCE RATING CHECKLIST

Answer Yes or No to the twenty questions below. Then rate your self-confidence using the rating scale at the end of the questionnaire.

	Yes	No
1. Do you feel nervous when you enter a room full of people, only a few of whom you know?	____	____
2. When you're at a meeting with people you don't know, are you afraid to voluntarily introduce yourself to others?	____	____
3. Does talking in public to a group of people frighten you?	____	____
4. Have you avoided trying a new job, hobby, or sport because you're afraid you might fail at it?	____	____
5. Is it difficult for you to make new friends?	____	____
6. Do you have trouble starting a conversation with strangers?	____	____

	Yes	No
7. Must you smoke a cigarette or hold a drink in order to feel relaxed in mixed company?	____	____
8. When you meet two or more people who stop talking as soon as they see you, do you immediately think they were talking about you?	____	____
9. Do you ever eavesdrop on the conversation of others, particularly those who might be talking about you?	____	____
10. Are you easily hurt by sarcasm or criticism?	____	____
11. Do you purposely seek praise or compliments much of the time?	____	____
12. Are you afraid to admit that you might have one or two minor faults?	____	____
13. Do you ever daydream about how you'll "get even" with someone who has "hurt" you?	____	____
14. When you fail at something you try, do you give up easily?	____	____
15. Do you feel bitter or resentful when some one else is praised or complimented in your presence?	____	____
16. Did you sulk for a day or more during the last month because someone else won a game, contest, or other competition?	____	____
17. Are you often envious or jealous of the success of your friends or associates?	____	____
18. Is it difficult for you to compliment others who have hit it big?	____	____
19. Do you feel uncomfortable and defensive when someone questions your knowledge or talent?	____	____
20. Do you "hold a grudge" for long periods against those people who criticize you?	____	____
Total Yes Checks	____	
Score = 5 × Number of Yes Checks	____	

Score	Your Self-Confidence Rating
0 to 20	Excellent; but work to remove those *yes* checks.
25 to 45	Good; but you could improve somewhat.
50 to 75	Poor; you *must* improve—this book will help you.
80 to 100	You really need help! But you have nowhere to go but up! So read on for that help.

Recognize the Results of Self-Confidence

Adequate self-confidence can make you rich quickly and surely. It can turn a discouraged, down-trodden failure into a glowing, happy success.

Phil D. called me at home one night, seeking advice. "Can you help me, Ty?" he wailed.

"I can help you if you want to help yourself," I replied.

"That I do," he said. "But I can't seem to get started."

"Phil," I said, "all you need to get started is a little self-confidence. Without a firm belief in yourself, and what you can do, you're lost."

Phil then told me his story. It was one I've heard thousands of times. The person starts in life with a momentary success of some sort—a profitable business deal, an outstanding career in school, a wonderful marriage, and so on. But then, for some reason, everything goes bad. Business deals fail, nobody wants the brilliant student, a marriage crashes on the rocks of a divorce court. The person is left shaken, discouraged, and frightened. *Where once he had a will to succeed he now almost has a will to fail!*

What can be done to convert failure to success? One powerful technique is to learn the five magic results of self-confidence and put these results to work in your life today.

"Phil," I said, "you have to regain your self-confidence. Once you do you can convert every failure to a success." Then I outlined the five magic results of self-confidence in a person's life. These five magic results are:

• Ability to build great riches fast

- Mastery of people—both men and women
- Control of your future
- Choice of happiness-giving leisure
- Ability, and funds, to help others

Put Self-Confidence to Work Today

"Now, Phil," I said, "I want you to *write down* those five magic results on a small card which you will keep in your wallet. Then, every time you open your wallet to get some money out, I want you to:

- Read the words on the card
- Repeat the words three times to yourself
- Resolve that you will become more self-confident

"If you do this your self-confidence will begin to zoom within five days," I told Phil.

"But must I go to all that trouble of writing it down?" Phil grumbled.

"Positively! You lose almost *all* the power of the method if you don't write out the five magic results of self-confidence. Further, you can't reinforce your thinking and emotions unless you *repeat* the five magic results for at least ten days."

Phil did as I said and came to see me a week later. He had a big smile on his face. "I feel great and I'm ready for action," he grinned. "What's next?"

"Fill this out," I said, passing him a piece of paper on which I had sketched the form below.

MY SELF-CONFIDENCE PROOFING KIT

To prove to myself that my self-confidence has increased, I will, by _____, do the following, using the five
              date
magic results of self-confidence given above. The sequence indicates my preferences for myself.

1. _____
2. _____
3. _____

4. _____
5. _____

Now what did Phil list? Here's a quick summary of his interests and preferences:

1. *Riches:* Build a fast fortune for myself.
2. *Mastery of people:* I want people to do *what* I say, *when* I tell them to do something.
3. *Help others:* I want to give money to charities which I believe are doing good work.
4. *Control my future:* I must be in command of what I do— I want to do things *my* way.
5. *Leisure:* My hobbies are important to me. I want to have time to pursue them.

Build Self-Confidence and Riches at the Same Time

Note that Phil's first interest was to build a fast fortune for himself. I was delighted to see this because:

Whenever a person builds a quick fortune, his self-confidences zooms with his income and he can reach all his other goals.

When the money is rolling in, I told Phil, everything else in life seems easy. So the first step we'll take is one that starts you on the road to *great* riches. Once you start earning big money your self-confidence will grow so fast that I may have to ask you to put the brakes on—so you don't become over-confident! Anyone who uses my methods can grow rich while he becomes more confident of himself, his abilities, and his handling of other people. Let's see how.

Pick Your Road to Wealth

To grow rich while building your self-confidence, you must know *how* you'd like to get rich. Do you want to:

- Sell to the general public
- Manufacture products

- Build houses, factories, offices
- Rent or trade real estate
- Invest in the stock market
- Be an industrial consultant
- Be any other type of wealth-builder?

If I were talking to you over lunch in a plush restaurant, as I do with many of my clients, I could determine within ten minutes exactly what you could do to grow wealthy while increasing your self-confidence. In a book such as this or any of my four other best-selling money books listed at the beginning of this book, it takes a little longer for you to decide how you want to grow rich.

Decide *now* which way you'd most enjoy getting rich. Write your intended way in the space below.

MY WEALTH RESOLVE

Today, _____, I firmly resolve to get rich by
　　　　　date

taking the following actions _____

_____

Take Your First Step to Riches

You now are ready to take your first step to riches and this is where your self-confidence takes over. "I know that," you say. "But what *is* my first step?"

For most people, the first step toward riches is getting started in a business of their own. That's the best way to hit it big today. Very few people reach the *big* money working for a company or other organization. So the first step toward wealth is one that takes piles of self-confidence. This step is: *Borrowing the money you need to acquire or start your own business.*

The longest journey begins with just one step. So too does your trip to the land of the big money begin with that first small step. You *can* take this step—and I want you to take that step as soon as possible.

Read Widely to Build Your Self-Confidence

To help you build the self-confidence you need to take your first step toward great wealth, here are some excellent books and publications that will positively show you how to increase your self-confidence. As you might expect, I firmly believe in the enormous power of books in motivating you to do more and in showing you how to improve your self-confidence quickly and surely. Buy, and read, as many of the following books as you can. You'll be glad you did!

Cerney—*Confidence and Power for Successful Living,* Parker Pub. Co.

Cerney—*Dynamic Laws of Thinking Rich,* Parker Pub. Co.

Hill and Stone—*Success Through a Positive Mental Attitude,* Prentice-Hall

Holland—*PRP: Key to Life on a Big Scale,* Parker Pub. Co.

Murphy—*Your Infinite Power to Be Rich,* Parker Pub. Co.

Parker Editorial Staff—*Parker Prosperity Program,* Parker Pub. Co.

Peale—*The Power of Positive Thinking,* Prentice-Hall

Ponder—*The Dynamic Laws of Prosperity,* Prentice-Hall

Rau—*Act Your Way to Successful Living,* Prentice-Hall

Schwartz—*The Magic of Thinking Big,* Prentice-Hall

Stone—*The Success System That Never Fails,* Prentice-Hall

Learn Where the Money Is

To obtain the money you need to make you rich, you must learn where the money is. This is easy! Just:

- Look for "Capital Available" ads in any large-city newspaper
- Visit local banks and ask who's lending money *now*
- Refer to the *Yellow Pages* in the phone book under the Financial and Mortgage headings
- Regularly read the monthly newsletter *International Wealth Success* which lists many money sources every

month of the year. (See below for instructions on how to subscribe to this newsletter.)

- Check the hundreds of money sources listed in my book *Business Capital Sources: How to Get Rich on Borrowed Money* available for $15 from IWS, Inc., P. O. Box 186, Merrick, N.Y. 11566
- Write to the Small Business Administration, Washington, D.C. 20244; ask for details of their lending program

Now I've just given you six ways of taking your first step toward wealth. What I want you to do *now* to prove to yourself that you *do* have the self-confidence you need to build a quick fortune is to *use all six ways of taking your first step!*

The first three steps, and the last, will cost you less than a dollar, plus a few minutes of your time. So you can't afford to say "No" to my advice! In fact, if you're so poor that you can't afford the few cents for a newspaper and postage stamp (your first and last steps) IWS is glad to air mail you the coins, just to get you started.

You can subscribe to the monthly newsletter *International Wealth Success* by sending $24.00 to IWS, Inc., P. O. Box 186, Merrick, N. Y. 11566. The book *Business Capital Sources: How to Get Rich on Borrowed Money* is available for $15 from the same address. It's a large volume full of money ideas and sources which you should find interesting and profitable.

Go Get Your Money

Once you've decided from whom you'll borrow your business capital, you'll have to appear for an interview. (If you don't like interviews with bankers or finance companies then I suggest that you read the above newsletter and book. Both list numerous *mail-order* lending organizations—places that lend money through the mail without a single interview.)

Your money interview will be your next step toward wealth *and* the next test of your renewed and improved self-confidence. If you can walk out of one or more interviews with the money in your pocket you will be on your way to an outstanding life of riches built on confident action and sound business judgment.

Put Action Behind Your Borrowed Money

Once you obtain your borrowed money—also called OPM, or *other people's money*—you are ready to put it to work. When you do you'll learn, and see at work, an important fact. This fact is:

> Money without action behind it is just paper. To make money earn money for you, you must put action behind the money.

Turn back to the Wealth Resolve you prepared earlier in this chapter. Read what you wrote there. That's what I had Phil, one of my many clients who turned to me for help, and about whom I was telling you earlier, do.

"What's your wealth resolve?" I asked Phil.

"Form an organization that will help people overcome their fear of flying and make a quick fortune at it," he replied.

I frowned—such a way of helping people while earning money had never occurred to me before. Yet the more I thought of it, the better the idea seemed.

"How much money do you need to start?" I asked Phil.

"Not much," he said. "A thousand dollars will do it, I think."

"Then go out and borrow it, using the hints I gave you."

Phil went to a local bank and within thirty minutes his loan for one thousand dollars was approved.

"Now you're ready for action—while you build your self-confidence," I said to Phil when he phoned me the good news.

"That I am," he laughed.

Get to Work—Now

"I'll start working right now," Phil said. "As soon as something develops I'll let you know."

Here's what Phil did to build a quick fortune while developing his self-confidence.

(1) Placed two small ads in big-city newspapers asking people who were afraid of flying to call him.

(2) Arranged a meeting for the callers in a rental meeting room in a local hotel.

(3) Drew up a program of activities designed to help people overcome their fear of flying—i.e., riding on commercial aircraft.

(4) Arranged with airlines to have members of his group tour airplanes parked on the ground to learn more about flying procedures, etc.

(5) Set up a membership fee structure.

(6) Arranged for a monthly publication carrying items that are interesting to his members.

Phil's club boomed. Soon he had branches throughout the country. The airlines, of course, were delighted. They bought advertising space in the club magazine, sent pilots to address club members, and made their aircraft available for inspection.

Within two years Phil's income from the club was more than $100,000 a year. "It's amazing how much self-confidence I have now," Phil said one day recently. "Now I never stop to think about self-confidence. I just go ahead and do whatever I want to. And, you know, somehow everything works out well!"

Look for the Best—and Get It

During my travels throughout the world I meet thousands of successful people. Of course, I also meet some unsuccessful people, too. One characteristic of unsuccessful people I've noted everywhere is that they look for the worst possible outcome in whatever they do. And, not surprisingly, they usually experience the worst possible results. This leads us to a helpful rule for building riches while increasing our self-confidence:

> Whenever you start a new activity, or re-direct an existing one, look for the best outcome; expect the best; and work hard at making the best result an actuality.

Expect the worst and that's what you'll usually get. Plan on the best, work to make the best a reality, and you'll usually obtain the best. Why settle for second-best when you deserve—and can get—the very best?

Know What You Want

Phil knew what he wanted in life—what he sought when I met him was a quick fortune using OPM. His desire to increase his self-confidence was only an incidental part of his over-all goal. Yet Phil recognized that without improving his self-confidence, his fortune goal would be much more difficult—or almost impossible —to achieve. This brings out a key fact:

> We all need specific goals to guide us in our search for wealth. Recognize this fact now; know what you want and you can obtain it.

Goals Give Your Life Direction

A person without goals is like a ship without a rudder, or an airplane without an engine. Without goals you wander through life, blown by this wind or that wind in the form of passing interests. Without *specific goals* you hop from one temporary interest to another, never devoting enough time to any one interest to convert it to hard cash.

Many of us delay in choosing goals because we lack self-confidence. We're afraid that if we choose a specific goal that we won't achieve it and our self-confidence will sink lower and lower.

Yet in recognizing these facts of human personality we should take courage because:

> Recognizing that we need goals in life is the first step toward choosing—and achieving—the goals that interest us. You really know what you want in life—all you lack is putting those wants into words.

Know what you want and you're more than half the way toward getting it. Let me show you why.

Four Who Achieved Their Money-Confidence Goals

In my consulting work with businessmen and clients, I meet hundreds of people every year who are trying to "hit it big," as they say. By "big" the person usually means *big money*. To show you that you truly can hit it big while improving your self-confidence, I'll give you four capsule actual case histories of people who did just that.

FROM BALDNESS TO RICHES

Barry B., a bald barber, could hardly support himself on his small income. And when it came to dates, Barry was worse off. His bald head embarrassed him and undermined what little self-confidence he had.

One day a customer asked Barry about a hair piece or toupee. Barry didn't know much about toupees but he promised his customer (and himself) to find out about them.

Barry immediately began an enthusiastic study of toupees. He soon found that toupees and wigs were selling at the rate of half a billion dollars per year. And before two weeks passed, Barry bought a toupee for himself. The change was instantaneous—in a moment Barry went from a middle-aged looking has-been to a nearly-under-thirty swinger.

Quickly Barry decided to become a toupee salesman in his barbershop. Soon his income tripled. And, as well, Barry found dates easy to find once his bald head was covered. Today Barry B. is married and owns an entire string of barber shops which specialize in toupees and hair pieces for their customers. Barry now has both self-confidence and money.

MAKING THE FISHING MARKET PAY OFF

Milton K., an engineer, was always full of bright ideas for new inventions. But Milt never put any of his ideas to work. Why? Because Milt was like a grasshopper—he jumped from one idea to the next without ever carrying one through to completion. The result? Milt, while creative and capable, lacked self-confidence. Further, his income was much lower than it should have been. What Milt needed to do, I told him, was "to stand still for a few days, weeks, or months, and put one idea into action."

Milt did just that—but I thought he was really asking for trouble. Why? Because Milt went into the outboard motor business at a time when even the giants of the industry were having problems. Starting in his backyard with just one volunteer helper, Milt built some 50 slim, lightweight outboard motors for fishermen. These motors sold out almost instantly. So Milt went back and built 200 more.

Today he's producing some 200 motors a day and can sell every one he builds. "When salesmen first saw my motor they wanted me to change its shape, put a gas tank on top, and build motors with more horsepower. But my customers liked the way it was. So I told the salesmen that I was building outboard motors for customers—not for salesmen. This was a big boost to my self-confidence when I was able to say that. But the boon to sales was even greater—I couldn't keep up with the orders. And as the orders have risen, so has my self-confidence."

Today Milt has a strong, healthy business with a big income. And his self-confidence is stronger every day. As Milt says, "I'm my own man and I love every minute of it!"

FROM SCHOOLROOM TO SOCIAL WORK

Rose L., a city school teacher, had all sorts of problems. They began with her job in a school populated by difficult-to-handle students. The "daily battle" as Rose called her teaching chores, was followed by problems at home— both her parents were elderly and ill. Her parents needed so much attention that Rose had little time for the social life she craved. So when Rose came to see me she was visibly distressed. "I've had it up to here," she said, placing one hand near the top of her forehead. "What can I do?"

We reviewed Rose's situation. "You must seek your happiness within your present world," I told Rose. "Until your parents are stronger, or until you can afford to pay someone to take care of them, you must accept the responsibilities you now have."

"I recognize that," Rose replied.

We worked out a program for Rose which included: (1) forming a recreation club for her students, (2) taking monthly trips to nearby interesting cities with her class, (3) presentation of weekly dancing, swimming, cooking, and other interesting courses in her school, and (4) part-time nursing help for her parents paid for by the club dues.

Within one month Rose found a new life within her old one. The club, trips, and lessons expanded her social life while enabling her to help her students. Further, Rose's parents began to improve their disposition and health as soon as they realized that their daughter would no longer be a built-in nursemaid to them.

Today Rose has enormous self-confidence and is much better off financially. Recently she married a wealthy widower she met in her club activities. Together with her husband, Rose plans to continue her club and outing activities for needy students throughout her state.

FROM SEAMAN TO TOP EXECUTIVE

Ben A. was an officer in the Merchant Marine. He sailed "on deck," as seamen say, as second mate. While Ben enjoyed going to sea while he was young, he found that he liked it less and less as the years passed. "I want to settle down, Ty," Ben said during our first talk. "This going to sea is for fish—not for me."

This conversation took place in a quiet seaman's pub on the west side waterfront of New York. I was grateful Ben came to see me because he helped me relive my many years at sea in the Merchant Marine.

"What would you rather do than go to sea?" I asked Ben.

"I'd rather be a big executive in an important business," Ben said.

"To become a big executive in an important firm in the New York area takes years of work, Ben," I said.

"I know that, Ty," he replied "and that's what's bugging me."

"Did you ever think of trying an overseas firm?" I asked Ben.

His eyes lit up. "Say, that's an excellent idea," Ben said. "I could be looking whenever I hit a foreign port."

"That's exactly it, Ben. And you'll find that you'll be welcome wherever you go. Many of today's wealthiest men —including Aristotle Onassis—got their start in a country other than their own. This approach to success is also a marvelous builder of your self-confidence. Because if you can make it overseas you make it anywhere."

"Just you watch me," Ben laughed.

Four months later the phone rang one evening about nine. It was Ben.

"I'm off to Rio as executive vice president of a large shipping outfit," Ben said happily. "They made me a beautiful offer—once I told them I might be available. The offer included everything a man might want—a big annual salary, stock options, profit sharing, a company Caddy, a city apartment, a boat, and so on. I really want to thank you for your help."

Today Ben is president of the shipping company. He's earning more than $100,000 per year and expects to reach $200,000 soon.

Think Like a Millionaire and Become One

There are hundreds of other real-life cases I could cite for you—ranging from a little old lady in the midwest who built a quick fortune ($1,000,000) on knitted sweaters, to a 24-year old youngster who made $3,000,000 in oil in three years. But each case would bring out the same basic principles for growing rich while increasing your self-confidence. These principles—which are really laws of life—are:

(1) Think rich to be rich. When you think rich you upgrade your self-confidence, your self-image, your energy. Start with your mind and watch the rest of yourself follow the lead.

(2) Act rich all the time. Put confidence and importance in your step, your manner, your voice. Watch how others look up to you for leadership and guidance.

(3) Take action toward your riches. Every morning when you awaken, ask yourself: *What will I do today to make myself richer?* And every time you do something, ask yourself: *Is this one more step on my road to riches?*

(4) Make time work for you. Plan ahead—with good planning you can have time for everything—riches, work, vacations, family, love, hobbies. Don't be victimized by time—instead, plan your time so it works for you.

(5) Set a goal and achieve it. Riches goals are the quickest milestones you can set for yourself. By making each goal specific, such as, *Open business by June 1,* you have definite deadlines to

aim for. And achieving your goal on schedule will make both your self-confidence and your income zoom.

(6) Dream your way to riches. Every night, before you go to sleep, and every day when you have a spare moment, dream your way to riches. How? Just imagine yourself succeeding enormously in different riches situations. See yourself applying for, and obtaining a loan you need, opening your first place of business, serving customers, opening a second place of business, and so on. Real life can be made from your dreams—and your dreams can truly make you as successful and as strong as you wish.

(7) Never give up your search for self-confidence and wealth It is *never* too late for increased self-confidence and greater wealth. You live with yourself *all* your life. And you become more interesting to yourself and others as your self-confidence and wealth increase. So start today—no matter what your age, young or not so young—to build your self-confidence while increasing your wealth.

two

Plotting Your
Wealth Future
Using Mind Power

Your brain contains more than three billion electrical circuits—more circuits than any computer that could ever be built, more circuits than all the telephone systems in all of North America. With such a tool at your command you can become richer than you ever dreamed possible.

How? By using your enormous mind power. Your mind is so fabulously powerful that you can easily put it to work earning your fortune. And do you know:

Both your mind, and your body will enjoy building great wealth. In fact the more riches you build, the happier you'll be!

Never Fear Mind Power

Some people—probably not you, but others—are afraid to think. They were so bruised in school by inept teachers who made thinking nasty work that they've never reached a tenth of their real potential in life. Are you one of these people? Use the following checklist to see.

MIND POWER CHECKLIST

	Yes	No
1. Do you avoid figures or numbers of any kind because they frighten you?	____	____
2. Are thinking-type card games difficult for you?	____	____
3. Is it difficult for you to concentrate on one subject for any sustained period?	____	____
4. Do you have difficulties when making out your income-tax form?	____	____
5. Are you a non-player when it comes to indoor games like chess, checkers, etc?	____	____

Score yourself 20 points for each "No" answer. If your score is less than 60, you could use your mind more actively to produce wealth for yourself. Why waste the enormous power you have at your command when this power is:

- Free to use
- Ready day and night
- Growing stronger every day
- More powerful than the biggest computer
- Health-giving and vital

There is no excuse for neglecting to use your wonderful "thinking engine." Read on to see how you can put your mind power to work with just a thought or a blink of your eyes!

Know What Your Mind Can Do for You

Your mind is much like an electronic computer. But your mind works much more efficiently than a computer. Further, your mind can perform many functions which a computer cannot.

From a fortune-building standpoint, your mind can:

- Select your money goals
- Choose ways to reach these goals
- Plan the steps to your future riches
- Anticipate potential problems for you

- Recognize problems when they occur
- Analyze problem causes
- Act to solve money and other problems
- Check the results of corrective actions

Your mind is very similar to what engineers call a feedback control system. The word *feedback* means that you:

(1) *Set* your desired result, i.e., your money goal
(2) *Take action*, i.e., start working toward your goal
(3) *Observe* results, i.e., count your income
(4) *Compare* results with your goals
(5) *Correct actions*, if necessary, to bring results in line with your goals
(6) *Continue* this process until you reach your goal, i.e., become rich

This six-step plan to wealth is unbeatable. And your mind knows exactly how to perform these six steps. To earn a quick fortune all most people need do is sharpen their money skills a bit. This chapter shows you how.

Sharpen Your Mind's Money Skills

As a test to show how your mind works, stop for a few moments and think of something which you believe is the most pleasant item you can think about, such as:

- A recent vacation you took
- How you felt when you won a prize for which you worked very hard
- The thrill of seeing your name in print
- The joy of learning that someone you love also loves you

Think for a minute or two about your pleasant topic. Then try to switch your mind to thinking about an extremely unpleasant topic, such as debts, poor health, loss of a loved one. Note how your mind resists being switched from the pleasant to the unpleasant.

So too, if you sharpen your mind's money skills, it will be

almost impossible to dull the sharp edge you develop. Here's how to sharpen your mind's money skills.

(1) Read several good books about money. Go to your local library and borrow three or four books on the general subject of money. Read these books carefully so you can learn more about the history of money, the place of money in our lives, and so on.

(2) Read several money-based self-help books. The books listed at the front of this book can give you a good start. Other useful self-help money books that I recommend you buy, read, and re-read are:

Business Capital Sources, $15, published by IWS Inc., P.O. Box 186, Merrick, New York 11566
How to Raise Money to Make Money, by William J. Casey, $39.95, Institute for Business Planning, 2 W. 13th Street, New York, New York 10011
Worldwide Riches Opportunities, $25, published by IWS Inc., P.O. Box 186, Merrick, New York 11566
A Handbook of Small Business Finance, 50 cents, Government Printing Office, Washington, D.C. 20402

(3) Read a good newspaper every day. Pay particular attention to the financial and business pages. When you read about a big business deal, imagine yourself as being in on the deal, negotiating a contract, holding out for a bigger cash down payment. Put yourself into the big money using free mental pictures which help you sharpen your money wits.

(4) Get interested in a specific business. Choose a business that interests you. Learn everything you can about the business—how much an owner earns, what expenses he has, what problems must be solved, and the like. Some day you may go into the business. Then your knowledge will come in handy. But even if you don't go into this business, you'll still be sharpening your money-making abilities for another business!

(5) Recognize that you have a mind and use it. Many beginning wealth-builders never think of their mind as a riches asset. This is sad because one of your greatest tools for wealth-building is your mind. So resolve, here and now, to mentally salute your mind every morning of your life. Then go out and put your mind to work earning your fortune.

Build Your ESP Power

Every successful businessman I've ever known—and that's thousands—could "read" people and situations. By that I mean he could sense:

- What people really want
- How much someone needs from a deal
- When a deal can be closed
- Where a business should be located
- Who was really important in a deal

This ability to read people and situations is easy to develop. Not only will it put money into your pocket, it will also improve your social life. And before you know it, people—your friends and family—will be saying you have the power of ESP—*extrasensory perception*.

Now please don't pooh-pooh ESP. Parts of the U.S. Government are spending thousands of dollars on ESP studies. And a good friend of mine borrowed $2,000 to start a consumer research firm because his reading of the situation was that big companies wanted to know what the public thought of their products. Seven years later he sold his firm for $11 million. That's not a bad return—only $11,000,000/7 = $1,571,428 per year! And, of course, he collected a big salary and had a nice big expense account during those seven years.

See What Others Think and Feel

You *can* "read" another person's thoughts, if you try to. Here's my seven-step plan for training yourself to "read" the thoughts of another person. When you want to know what others think and feel:

(1) Give the other person your complete attention.
(2) Stop any thoughts of what *you* want.
(3) Watch the other person carefully.
(4) Observe the other person's face and hands.
(5) Be alert for invisible signals in the air.

(6) Say what you think these signals tell you.

(7) Keep probing for greater accuracy.

Let's look at this system in action. Then you'll understand each step better.

Carl C. came to my office to talk over a business he was interested in. We sat facing each other.

I looked at Carl (Step 1) and thought only of him (Step 2) and his business interest. Watching Carl carefully (Step 3), I could see that he was telling me most of his story, but not *all*. How did I know this? I could see a nervous lip and hand motion (Step 4).

Then I began to feel *invisible* signals in the air between us (Step 5). The air seemed to vibrate, transmitting to me Carl's unspoken need.

"You need money to start this business, Carl," I said. "And you want me to lend it to you. Right?" (Step 6)

"How'd you guess that?" Carl asked with a sigh of relief. "You sent me the signal," I answered. "Now how much do you need?" (Step 7)

Carl needed $1,000 to go into the snowmobile business. I lent him the money with a request that I be cut in for a piece of the action—i.e., a part of the profits.

Starting in his garage with just a few local youths as after-school helpers, Carl built his business so fast that he couldn't get parts quickly enough to fill orders. Three years after borrowing that $1,000 Carl sold his snowmobile business for $3 million. My "piece of the action" cut on that sale, was I assure you, a trifle more than $1,000!

Read Those Signals Right

The big moment of truth in ESP comes when two people are talking—one acting as the *sender* or *transmitter* of signals, much like a radio or TV station in your local area, and the other as the *receiver*, such as your home radio or TV. When you're trying to "read" the other person you are the receiver. To receive the transmitted signals clearly, you must have all your antennae at the ready.

To receive clearly and accurately:

(1) Wipe out all thoughts of what *you* want.
(2) Give your entire attention to the other person.
(3) Listen, and watch, for the signals being sent to you.
(4) Wait until the other person grows silent.
(5) Then *ask* if the signal you perceive is the signal being sent.
(6) Carefully listen to the reply. If it's *Yes*, you know you read correctly. But if the answer is *No*, listen for any other information supplied you. It may give you the answer you seek.
(7) Keep trying if your first reading is not correct.

Put Profits in Your ESP

Your big moment in reading the thoughts of others comes just before the other person falls silent. It is then, in my opinion, that the thought transfer forces are the strongest. Let me show you why.

I was discussing a big business deal—in the $1 million range—with an extremely successful, wealthy, and well-educated man. In such a situation it may be extremely difficult to shut out all thoughts except those concerned with the other person and the business deal at hand.

To overcome any bias that I might have because this was not an ordinary business conversation, i.e.,

- The deal was big
- The other person was different from the usual business associate
- Outside factors could mislead me,

I took an important step. I shut my eyes behind my upheld hand and listened, concentrating on what was said.

As I listened I noted that the words began to come more and more slowly. At the same time—*even though my eyes were tightly shut*—I began to feel strong thoughts that this gentleman wanted the business deal to be put under contract immediately. His thought waves increased in strength until they almost shouted at me "Offer me a contract now and I'll sign it."

Keeping my eyes shut, I continued to listen. Then he stopped talking. At that instant his thought waves were so strong that I felt our minds were talking a special language which was crystal clear to both of us.

"Would you like me to prepare a contract covering the deal?" I *asked*.

"Oh yes, Ty," he breathed. "That's exactly what I had in mind. How could you have guessed?"

"Simply by listening," I felt like saying, but I didn't.

There's at least a million dollars worth of ESP profits in your mind *right now*. You can make those profits yours quickly and easily—if you use the rules I gave you above.

Get More from Your Thought Power

The incident I just related to you points up some other powerful ESP techniques. These are:

(1) When outside interference gets in the way of clear thinking, shut your eyes.

(2) Hear only the voice of the speaker.

(3) Be alert for the thought waves. They'll come to you whether your eyes are open or closed.

(4) Ask—don't tell—if your thought reading is correct.

Use these techniques and you'll multiply your ESP thought power by ten times or more. Remember this:

To make ESP pay you a big income you must be super-sensitive to the other person. So start developing your sensitivity today.

Long-Distance Mind Power Will Work for You Too

A good friend of mine, Andy D., owns a freight airline. Recently, while having lunch in New York, Andy thought he heard, in his mind's "ear," a crash and saw, in his mind's "eye," one of his planes dive into the water while making a landing approach. He brushed aside the picture he'd heard and seen in his mind as a stray, unimportant thought.

When Andy returned to his office his secretary was weeping. "What's wrong, Claire?" Andy asked.

"Read this," she sobbed handing him a yellow cablegram. His eyes bulged as he read:

FLIGHT 273 CRASHED INTO BAY ON HONG KONG LANDING APPROACH STOP NO SURVIVORS STOP AIRCRAFT AND CARGO APPEAR TOTAL LOSS STOP   HONG KONG AGENT

"What happened to the crew?" was Andy's first thought. Immediately the answer came to him in the form of a picture. In his mind's eye—like on a black-and-white TV screen—Andy saw the broken and twisted cockpit at the bottom of the bay. Three bodies —the entire crew—were trapped inside the cockpit by the canted seats and the shattered sides of the fuselage.

"And the cargo?" Andy asked himself. Another picture immediately flashed in Andy's mind. This picture showed the main body of the big four-engine jet lying on the bottom of the bay, split open by a long jagged cut from end to end. Miraculously, the cargo was intact, still strapped down to the fuselage floor.

"Get me on the first flight to Hong Kong," Andy shouted to Claire. "And be sure my scuba equipment is packed."

Two days later Andy dove to the wreck of his freight plane. "Everything, Ty," he told me later, "was exactly as I saw it in my mind in the office—the cockpit, the bodies of the crew, the cargo. I was really broken up by the loss of the crew, but there was nothing I could do about it, too much time had passed. But we were able to salvage the entire cargo. I gave a big contribution to each of the crewmen's families. Each family also received a large insurance payment, so I'm convinced that they're all well cared for. But if those pictures hadn't come to me, I'd have gone broke because the cargo would have been lost."

There you have it. Thought pictures that traveled 12,000 miles and saved a big business investment. While Andy said he would have gone broke from the accident, I'm sure he would have recovered quickly.

Now why can't you use such thought pictures in your business? You can—and I want you to start doing so right now. Here's how.

Six Rules for Seeing Thought Pictures

Here are six rules for seeing thought pictures in your business activities.

1. Don't expect perfection—many of the pictures you see will be shadowy, not quite clear (much like black-and-white TV).
2. Shut your eyes and open your ears—either physically or figuratively so you hear clearly what the speaker is attempting to say to you.
3. Remember that many of the messages you receive come from the subconscious of the speaker. These messages haven't yet reached his conscious level (i.e., he has yet to recognize them) yet you can read them!
4. Be receptive to every thought—you can't expect to win friends if you dislike people!
5. Don't be alarmed by strange thoughts you may receive—the capacity of the human mind is enormous and people have all kinds of ideas and feelings.
6. Try hardest when you feel the thought waves coming to you. This is when you should receive the clearest pictures and obtain the most information.

Yes, you can receive long-distance money pictures if you use the power of your mind. Put the above six rules to work for yourself and you're certain to earn a big fortune.

Multiply Your Mind-Magic

The word *mind* begins with the letter *M* and this letter is the key to multiplying your mind-magic. And what is mind-magic?

Mind-magic is the unlimited power you have in your mind to produce ideas, innovations, and improvements that can make you rich and happy.

Your mind is loaded with magic power to:

• Make more money • Multiply your skills

- Motivate anyone
- Move people
- Mesmerize others
- "Magnetize" thoughts
- Meditate on wealth

- Memorize details
- Manipulate facts, figures
- Mechanize work
- Magnify your ideas
- Memorize details

Note that each of these magic power words begins with the same letter as the words mind and money. Magic mind power can bring you much more money than you now have—if you'll just work a little to allow this marvelous power to come into your life. By recognizing what mind-magic is, you are way ahead of those people who don't know it exists. Let's put your mind-magic to work right now!

Mind-Magic Can Make You Rich

You are now about to demonstrate for yourself just how powerful your mind is. If you don't know the power of your mind, the results of this demonstration will astound you. And if you do know, the results will reassure you.

MIND-MAGIC DEMONSTRATION

1. List here four new money ideas you've had recently.
   A. _____   C. _____
   B. _____   D. _____
2. Manipulate each idea in your mind until you can see how *you* can make money from the idea. List here how much money you might make from each of the four ideas.
   A. _____   C. _____
   B. _____   D. _____
3. Now *massage* each idea—that is, work it over in your mind until you can at least double the money you might make from each idea. List, briefly, how you'd multiply your money-making.
   A. _____   C. _____
   B. _____   D. _____
4. Make a mind-magic resolution—here and now—which will motivate you into making your money dreams come true. Enter below the date on which you plan to start *making money* from each idea.

A. _____   C. _____
B. _____   D. _____

5. Monitor your money plans by checking up on your progress at regular intervals. Mark below the dates on which you will monitor each money plan.

A. ____ ____ ____   C. ____ ____ ____
B. ____ ____ ____   D. ____ ____ ____

6. Keep using your mind-magic to develop new ideas. List below *six* new money ideas you've developed since you first started using your mind-magic power.

1. _____   4. _____

2. _____   5. _____

3. _____   6. _____

Quadruple Your Income Using Mind-Magic

Chet K. was struggling along on an income of $6,000 per year. "If I could only make $20,000 a year," Chet said, "I'd really be clear of all my problems."

"That's easy, Chet," I replied. "Just do as I say and you'll easily quadruple your income."

"I'll believe it when I have the money in my hands," Chet laughed.

"That won't be long," I said. Here's what I had Chet do. And I want you to do the same—if you'd like to quadruple your income using mind-magic. Take these ten steps.

1. *Believe you can quadruple your income* using mind-magic. (If you don't believe, try for a few weeks to forget your disbelief while you allow your mind-magic to work.)

2. *Write on a slip of paper* your present yearly income. Multiply this number by four and write the result on the paper below the first number. (Thus, Chet wrote $6,000 and $24,000 on his slip of paper.)

3. *List three ways* you could quadruple your income. Thus, you might list the following: (a) Start, and be a success in, my own business. (b) Be promoted to president of the company for which I work. (c) Earn a big spare-time income.

4. *Study each way thoroughly* for at least eight hours. List the advantages and disadvantages of each way of quadrupling your income. *Write* these pros and cons on the same slip of paper on which you marked your present and expected earnings.

5. *Trade off the pros and cons*—that is, cross out one pro which you believe balances or equals one con. Continue this until you can't cross out any more on a one-for-one basis. Then shift to a 2-for-1, 3-for-1, and so on basis for either pro or con.

6. *Pick the best way for you*—i.e., the way having the largest number of *pros* or advantages remaining. This probably will be the way which has the least number of cons, or disadvantages, remaining.

7. *Concentrate on the best way*—that is, stop thinking about the other ways you considered earlier. Explore every idea you can get concerning the way you think you can best quadruple your income.

8. *Make comprehensive notes*—write down every thought that comes to you from your mind-magic. Because *it is your mind-magic,* you know, that is feeding good, money-laden ideas into your brain. Writing down your ideas will help you remember the good ones.

9. *Buy a small ruled notebook* that will fit in your pocket. Transfer all your notes to this book. Classify each note under a major category before entering it in a section of your notebook devoted to just this one classification.

10. *Start working on your best way* to quadruple your income. Make notes of interesting facts, prices, sales, and the like in your notebook. Keep pushing every day of every week. Don't let up. Soon, you'll see, your income will double, triple, and then quadruple.

Set Your Second Mind to Work

Each of us has a conscious mind and a subconscious mind—which I prefer to call your "second mind." Your conscious mind is the one you use every day to:

- Solve business problems
- Make decisions
- Compute prices, salaries, etc.

Your subconscious mind, or second mind, works around the clock for your conscious mind, feeding information to it, receiving information. But the big difference between your conscious mind and your second or subconscious mind is:

You are unaware of the working of your subconscious mind. It labors for you day and night and can produce your biggest and most profitable ideas.

To set your second mind to work quickly and efficiently:

(1) Recognize that you have a powerful subconscious mind.
(2) Resolve today to use the enormous reservoirs and power of your subconscious mind.
(3) Regularly "drop" into your subconscious mind a business or money problem you may have.
(4) Turn away from the problem—that is, ignore it for awhile.
(5) Observe if the answer or solution comes to you like a "flash"—it often will.

The answer that occurs to you while you're walking along the street, watching TV, or doing something else completely unrelated to the problem is the work of your subconscious mind. And some of the results you obtain from your subconscious mind will be so remarkable that you will term them "mind-magic," for that is what they truly are.

Create Mental Pictures of Your Wealth

One picture is worth a thousand words, says the ancient proverb. I extend this proverb to say:

One mental picture of your future wealth is worth at least one thousand hours of extra work.

In talking with wealthy men around the world, I've often noticed that many of these men have exceptionally strong powers of visualization. They can "see" in their minds the successful completion of every job or task they plan. Also, they can see their bank account as it gets bigger and bigger.

Why Mental Pictures Pay Off

When you dream through your mind's eye you build an enormous drive within yourself to accomplish your objective. Wealthy men have often said to me:

"It was a lot easier to make my first million than I visualized."

And

"I saw the whole deal in my mind's eye before it even started. The deal went off exactly as I visualized it would."

And

"I plan every deal—step by step. I try to figure every angle in advance. Then nothing happens that surprises me because I solve my problems in my mind before they really occur!"

And

"There's no substitute for the dry run in your mind. For example, I review every possible item that might come up in a loan interview *before* I have the interview. I have the answers to the questions before the loan officer asks them. No loan application of mine was ever refused!

Yes, mental pictures can make you wealthy. Just use them as we've recommended here and you can't go wrong. Combined with the other approaches given you in this chapter, mental pictures can be the most powerful wealth tool you'll ever find!

Now here are some extremely useful books for your mind-magic library. These books will help you understand yourself and other people better. Read as many of these books as you can.

USEFUL BOOKS ON PSYCHIC POWER

Allen—*Morphological Creativity: The Miracle of Your Hidden Brain Power*, Prentice-Hall

Bradley and Bradley—*Psychic Phenomena: Revelation and Experience,* Parker Pub. Co.

Brennan—*Make the Most of Your Hidden Mind Power,* Prentice-Hall

Bristol—*Magic of Believing,* Prentice-Hall

Conklin—*The Power of a Magnetic Personality,* Parker Pub. Co.

De Mente—*Face Reading for Fun and Profit,* Parker Pub. Co.

Edwards—*Psycho-Recording: Secrets of Mental Vision,* Prentice-Hall

Finley—*Mental Dynamics: Power Thinking for Personal Success,* Prentice-Hall

Frantz—*The Miracle Success System: A Scientific Way to Get What You Want in Life,* Parker Pub. Co.

Hersey—*How to Cash in on Your Hidden Memory Power,* Prentice-Hall

Howard—*Mystic Path to Cosmic Power,* Parker Pub. Co.

Howard—*Psycho-Pictography: The New Way to Use the Miracle Power of Your Mind,* Parker Pub. Co.

Howard—*Secrets of Mental Magic,* Prentice-Hall

Jacobsen—*The Power of Your Mind,* Parker Pub. Co.

Maltz—*The Magic Power of Self-Image Psychology: The New Way to a Bright, Full Life,* Prentice-Hall

Manning—*Helping Yourself with ESP,* Parker Pub. Co.

Murphy—*Amazing Laws of Cosmic Mind Power,* Parker Pub. Co.

Murphy—*Miracle of Mind Dynamics,* Parker Pub. Co.

Murphy—*The Power of Your Subconscious Mind,* Parker Pub. Co.

Norvell—*Meta-Physics: New Dimensions of the Mind,* Parker Pub. Co.

Peale—*The Power of Positive Thinking,* Prentice-Hall

Petrie and Stone—*How to Strengthen Your Life with Mental Isometrics,* Parker Pub. Co.

Ponder—*The Prosperity Secret of the Ages,* Parker Pub. Co.

Schwartz—*The Magic of Psychic Power,* Parker Pub. Co.

Simmons—*Dynamic Personal Power for You,* Parker Pub. Co.

Van Fleet—*How to Use the Dynamics of Motivation,* Parker Pub. Co.

Williams—*The Knack of Using Your Subconscious Mind,* Prentice-Hall

Williams—*The Wisdom of Your Subconscious Mind,* Prentice-Hall

Young—*Cyclomancy: The Secret of Psychic Power,* Parker Pub. Co.

Young—*The Laws of Mental Domination: How to Master and Use Them for Dynamic Life Force,* Parker Pub. Co.

Young—*The Secrets of Personal Psychic Power,* Parker Pub. Co.

three

Improving Your Health While Building Your Wealth

You may have heard people say "All the wealth in the world isn't worth anything without your health." And I agree one hundred percent. But I claim that it isn't necessary to lose your health to make big money. Instead, I see your fortune-building activities as improving your health!

Why Health and Wealth Rhyme

Hard work is good for your body, your mind, and your bank account. Why? Because hard work:

- Improves your muscles
- Keeps your body tuned up
- Builds an alert mind
- Sharpens your perception
- Increases your reserve strength
- Widens your friendships
- Spurs you on to greater achievements

45

So wealth activities can lead to improved health—if you're careful not to overdo anything. This means you must:

- Relax regularly
- Limit stimulants
- Find happiness in your work
- Avoid worry
- Exercise daily
- Have regular physical checkups
- Smile and laugh as often as possible

Enjoy what you do, work at a comfortable pace, and take care of your body. Follow this rule and you'll grow in health while you grow in wealth.

Stopping Work Can Damage Your Health

At least a dozen friends and business associates of mine retired before they were forty-five years old. Several retired at age thirty-eight. One retired at thirty.

The plans these men had varied from all-day golf matches every day to round-the-world cruises. Yet every one of these early retirees was back to work within a year, or less, after he retired. Why? Because:

Early retirement while a person is still in his prime can lead to mental and physical problems. It is often more unhealthy not to work than to work!

When you slow down mentally and physically at an early age you lose the drive that keeps your mind alert and your health at its peak.

So forget early retirement! Concentrate instead on becoming an early millionaire who will:

- Create a worthwhile business
- Enjoy money
- Help the needy
- Keep busy and active as long as possible

Try My Magic Health Formula

You are probably reading this book because you think the author may have one or two good ideas for you. I hope that I do! Many readers of my other books say they get good ideas from them.

Here's a business health idea which I hope you find helpful. It has, I know, been an enormous help to me. This idea is:

Every morning when you wake up, repeat to yourself the word SHEEN and think of the meaning of each letter in the word:

   S = smile as you start your day
   H = happiness will be yours
   E = exercise will keep your body trim
   E = enthusiasm will keep your mind fit
   N = new ideas and people will keep you young

This word SHEEN works magic for many of the people who come to me for help. By repeating the word and thinking of the meaning of each letter you, early in the day:

- Begin by smiling
- Set your mind on happiness
- Remind yourself of exercise
- Stimulate your enthusiasms
- Seek the new and exciting

This is a good way for starting any day—no matter what your job or business may be. Combined with the other ideas in this chapter, you will have a powerful technique for building your health while you gather wealth!

Combine Health and Wealth

Danny M. had a very bad stomach condition. He knew every kind of stomach pain there was. As the years went by, Danny's pains became worse. No doctor or medicine seemed to be able to help.

"How often do you think of your stomach?" I asked Danny when he came to me. "All the time," he said mournfully. "So would you if it were your stomach."

(I didn't tell Danny that at the age of 19 I had almost been shipped to the cemetery because of a perforated stomach ulcer. He couldn't tell me much about stomach pains that I didn't know.)

"Danny," I said, "what you need is an interest in something that is so strong that it takes your mind out of your stomach and puts it back in your head. Certainly I'm not a doctor but I do know that the less you worry about your body, the better it usually works. So if we can get you thinking about something constructive and profitable, your stomach just might like it!"

Here's what I had Danny do.

(1) List his major business interests.
    They were mail order, education, and helping others.
(2) Name several businesses he liked.
    These were correspondence courses, teaching, and writing articles.
(3) Pick his favorite hobbies.
    These were writing, boating, and fishing.

Without realizing it Danny had written himself into business. Why? Well look at his first and second choices shown above. They are:

- Mail order
- Education
- Correspondence courses
- Teaching
- Writing
- Boating

"Danny," I said, "you ought to teach boating by mail."

"Don't be funny," Danny said in an annoyed tone, "my stomach couldn't stand it."

"Forget your stomach and get to work," I replied somewhat peevishly. "You have nothing to lose but your bellyache!"

Turn Your Pains into Gains

Danny went away and I didn't hear from him for two months. One day the phone rang. "Ty," Danny said happily, "I'm about to launch my first boating correspondence course."

"Great," I said. "I wish you the best of luck."

"I decided to turn my pains into gains," Danny said somewhat sheepishly. "Already my gut feels better."

"Keep me informed about your gains—not your pains," I laughed.

Danny introduced his correspondence course to the boating public. It was an immediate success, even though a number of competitors were active in the field. Today Danny has four courses booming along.

"How's your tummy?" I asked him recently.

"I forgot I had one," he laughed. "The best medicine I ever took was to get interested in something outside my stomach. It might not work for everyone but it sure worked for me. I haven't been to the doctor in two years! He's astounded by my cure."

Draw Your Health Profile

You're healthier than you think! I'll show you why. Just fill out the accompanying personal health profile right now. Be as objective as possible when rating your health as excellent (E), good (G), average (A), or poor (P).

PERSONAL HEALTH PROFILE

Part of Body	Present Health			
Eyes	E	G	A	P
Ears	E	G	A	P
Nose	E	G	A	P
Mouth	E	G	A	P
Neck	E	G	A	P
Chest	E	G	A	P

Part of Body	Present Health
Heart	E G A P
Lungs	E G A P
Stomach	E G A P
Legs	E G A P
Arms	E G A P
Feet	E G A P
Hands	E G A P
Others:	
_____	E G A P
_____	E G A P
_____	E G A P

Circle that letter which indicates your general health for each part of your body. Then connect the circles with a solid line—your health profile. Now study your general health condition this way.

- The further left your health profile, the healthier you are, in your opinion.
- With a central profile your health is average, in your opinion.
- A far right profile indicates that you believe your health is poor.

Make Health Your Wealth Goal

Today millions of people swim, jog, walk, golf, and run just to improve their health. Some big business firms have daily exercise breaks for their executives and office workers. (One of the funniest sights you'll ever see is a big executive chinning himself on the bar over the door of his plush office.)

If these millions of people are willing to exercise strenuously just to keep in shape, why shouldn't you be willing to make health your wealth goal? When you do this you make big money while you strengthen your health! Here's how:

(1) Visit your doctor.

(2) Have him give you a physical checkup.

(3) Tell him of your health and wealth plans.

(4) Ask him what you can do in your wealth efforts to improve your health.

(5) Build your wealth efforts around your doctor's recommendations.

From Wheelchair to Riches in a Year

Laura C. was confined to a wheelchair by a muscular disorder. For months her doctor tried to convince Laura that she should leave her wheelchair for an hour or so a day and walk about on crutches. The exercise on the crutches would, the doctor hoped, help to rebuild Laura's muscles so she could once again walk. But Laura refused, fearing she would fall and injure herself.

One day, while idly watching TV, Laura saw a group of handicapped people playing basketball from their wheelchairs. The game was fast and furious, and intensely interesting.

After the game the coach of the winning team was interviewed. "I was once in a wheelchair myself," he told the announcer. "But I decided that I could, and would, get out of it. Before I knew what I'd done, I was walking again. Now I hope to get some of my players walking, too."

This statement made Laura think. Perhaps she, too, could get out of her wheelchair and walk again. What she needed, Laura told herself, was an interest in something which would take her right out of her wheelchair.

Laura's interest came the next day in the form of an ad she received from the monthly newsletter *International Wealth Success*. The ad told her that she could make money at home in a number of different activities—export-import, mail order, tutoring, consulting, and so on. Since Laura had once been a teacher, she decided to subscribe to the IWS Newsletter for one year by sending $24 to IWS at P.O. Box 186, Merrick, N.Y. 11566, and to try tutoring, as the newsletter suggested.

Placing a few small ads in the local papers by phone the next day, Laura was stunned by the number of people who wanted, or needed, private tutoring. What Laura hadn't realized was that thousands of people had enough money to pay for specialized instructions which interested them, or which they needed. Within three days Laura was out of her wheelchair and walking *without* her crutches.

Take Action Fast to Acquire Health with Wealth

Laura's first step after leaving her wheelchair was to list the kinds of tutoring people sought. Her list included:

- Slow-learning students
- Professional people seeking licenses
- Hobbyists wanting to increase their skill
- Business people trying to update their knowledge

What Laura didn't realize at the time was that she had stumbled onto an enormous market—a market which is called *continuing education*. There are millions of people throughout the world today who have a *need* to learn new subjects and new techniques.

Laura sensed that she could hit it big in a hurry if she acted quickly. So within a week Laura:

- Advertised for teachers
- Hired 12 teachers
- Placed free and paid ads for courses
- Rented several classrooms
- Began collecting tuition

Her tutoring classes boomed instantly. Within just one year after leaving her wheelchair, Laura was earning more than $150,000 per year from her tutoring.

What happened to her wheelchair and crutches? She donated them to the local hospital. And the last time I spoke to Laura she was radiant and happy. Why? Because *she* was being tutored—she was taking dancing lessons to strengthen her leg muscles and widen her social life.

Listen to Your Doctor But Make Money!

Visit your doctor when you feel the need. Follow his directions—don't take chances with your health. But make money at the same time! How?

(1) Work out, within the habit pattern your doctor gives you, a plan for earning *big* money.

(2) Put your plan into *action.*

(3) Have your *health* checked regularly.

(4) Concentrate on *money* while emphasizing health.

(5) Check your money and health *progress* regularly.

(6) Keep pushing until you achieve your *goal.*

Never neglect your health. At the same time, never forget what money can give you:

* Independence
* Peace of mind
* Beautiful home
* Vacation travel
* Happy retirement
* Anything else you want

Build Riches Anywhere

Sidney L. was told to move to the southwest to cure a lung condition. The news nearly shattered Sidney because he had never been outside a big city during his life. Yet he couldn't forget the words of his doctor: "You won't live more than six months if you stay in this damp northern climate."

So though he had much fear in his heart, Sid moved himself and his family to the dry climate of Tucson, Arizona. Since he was making such a complete break with the past, Sid decided to try to start a new business or job in the city that he'd picked after asking his doctor for advice on the best spot for his health.

In Tucson, Sid saw that he could sell tourist trinkets, pump gas into autos, or do any of several similar jobs. But none of these interested him, so Sid kept looking.

Late one evening Sid asked himself: "What really interests me?" Instantly the answer came to him—money. "Then why not concentrate on money," he said to himself.

The next day Sid came upon an ad which read:

Become a Financial Broker, Finder, and Business Broker-Consulant. Take our course and learn what you need to know. This course includes a:

- Big book of hundreds of financial sources
- Typical loan application forms
- Announcements of your new business for free publicity
- Other useful broker information
- Four handsome certificates for your office

Send $99.50 for your course to IWS, Inc., P.O. Box 186, Merrick, N. Y. 11566.

Sid sensed that this course might give him the answer he needed. So he sent the money and quickly received his course. The course was exactly what he needed because:

- He could study at home whenever he had time
- There were no lessons to send in—the answers came with the course
- The instructions were specific, in step-by-step form
- His four certificates were a handsome addition to his den
- It took only another $35 or so to go into business (letterheads, postage, etc.)
- He could finish the reading part of the course in three days

Put Your Know-how to Work

Within a week after receiving his course Sid was in business. And the first day he was in business Sid learned one key lesson. This was:

Every business he visited or called on needed money. It didn't make any difference whether the business was large or small—the ready availability of money gave him immediate entry for an interview.

Sid was delighted and resolved to arrange as many loans as possible during the coming month. On each loan Sid would earn a:

- Commission from *both* the lender and borrower
- Finder's fee from either the lender or borrower, or or both, if such a fee was offered by either group

• Brokerage fee when a business was bought or sold as
part of the deal

During his first month in business Sid worked 22 days and
arranged 14 loans. His total commissions and fees on these 14
loans was $15,308.91. Thus, Sid earned almost $700 per day
during his first month in business.

Of course, Sid worked hard. Further, he was in a new location, and forced to make good because of his health condition.
Other people trying to start as financial brokers might not be as
successful. But their chances in this outstanding profession of
financial broker, finder, business broker-consultant, are excellent
because so few people have taken the time to study how to make
good in the profession.

Become Your Own Money Source

As a financial broker, finder, business broker-consultant you
soon learn:

• Which organizations will pay you money to find them
someone to lend money to
• Who's looking for firms and people to lend money to
• Who has money to lend
• Who needs money
• Who wants to acquire, merge, or sell a business
• Who needs a consultant

Knowing who has money to lend is valuable information to
you, both in your business and in new activities you may select.
By this I mean you become your own financial broker!

That's exactly what Sid did, once he established himself as
a financial broker, finder, business broker-consultant. Since it
took only a few hours a day—four or less—to run his financial
business, Sid decided to open a trailer park in a nearby city.
This is the way Sid worked his deal. He:

(1) Located a suitable piece of land.
(2) Borrowed all the cash he needed for the down payment
and improvements.
(3) Purchased the land.

(4) Had the improvements made (sewers, roads, fences, electricity, etc.).

(5) Rented out space on the land.

(6) Made one of his tenants the landlord.

(7) Collected a profit from the land to pay off his loan.

(8) Held the land while it appreciated in value.

Aim at Capital-Gain Profits

Sid expanded his trailer-park business until he had six parks. Then he decided to sell his parks and go into the travel business.

So Sid sold all six trailer parks at whopping capital-gains profits. This means that his income tax was lower than for ordinary income. It also means that Sid:

- Took over property using borrowed money
- Earned a profit from the property while paying off his loan
- Sold the property at a handsome profit

This is a system that can't be bettered by the average man. In one-word summary form of this system you:

- Find
- Borrow
- Buy
- Profit
- Repay
- Sell
- Profit
- Repeat

And if you want, you can skip the last three steps. But either way, you can make big profits on other people's money, just as Sid did!

Be a Big Winner in the Health-Wealth Game

Hundreds of people in my business circles have overcome intense and serious physical and mental ailments by finding new and profitable interests. Here are a few of these people and brief details of how they hit it big in the health-wealth game.

Ailment	Business Activity
Heart disease	Ownership and operation of a group of hobby shops
Tuberculosis	Ski-lodge operation
Stomach ulcer	Management consulting firm
Arthritis	Mail-order business in home
Blindness	Telephone-answering service operation
Lower-body paralysis	Limousine service for suburban areas
Inner-ear infections	Theatre-ticket agency
Arm amputation	Metal fabrication shop
Lung problems	Travel agency ownership and operation
Gland enlargement	Boat chartering service
Asthma	Financial broker, finder, business broker-consultant
Tumors	Picture-framing business operation

Now I am NOT saying that the business interests of these men and women cured their ailments. That must be clearly understood.

Further, *I do NOT recommend that anyone with one or more of the listed ailments go into the business listed. You MUST follow your doctor's advice!*

But I *DO* say the following about these happy, successful people:

- Their business interests *appeared* to relieve their health problems
- As their incomes increased, they could afford better, and more frequent, medical care
- None of these people died at work
- All appeared happier and healthier after getting interested in a business of their own
- All are wealthier today than when their health was poor

- All are healthier today than when they were ill
- All seem to be better occupied in their business than they were when preoccupied with their health problems

Take Off Now for Better Health, Greater Wealth

You can start making your health better today while you begin building your wealth. There's no need to remain sickly, poor, unloved, and full of pain. So resolve, here and now that you will:

- Get healthy soon
- Earn riches fast
- Find someone to love
- Build more and more wealth
- Grow stronger every day
- Help others who need help
- Continue to grow in strength, riches, and wisdom day by day

There is no reason why every reader of this book shouldn't become healthier and wealthier before he or she is a month older.

Both health and wealth depend, to a large extent, on your mental attitude. Form the right mental attitude and you've taken a giant step forward on your way to both glorious health and enduring wealth. To form the right mental attitude for better health:

(1) Apply the SHEEN formula given earlier.
(2) Tell yourself daily that you will become healthier.
(3) Get the *best* medical advice you can—and follow it.
(4) Don't try to kid your doctor—do as he says.
(5) Exercise within your capabilities and in accordance with your doctor's recommendations.
(6) Seek *health*—not sickness.
(7) *Feel* healthy—breathe deeply; use your muscles; use your mind; make your body work for your wealth.

To form the right mental attitude for greater wealth:

(1) Daily tell yourself that you will become wealthy. (If one of every thousand people in the United States can be a millionaire, so can you!)

(2) Pick your road to wealth and follow it.

(3) Never give up your desire *and* drive for wealth—giving up won't get you anywhere.

(4) Push onward every day—tell yourself that wealth will bring you health—build wealth to attain health.

(5) Tell yourself every hour of every day that (a) you are great; (b) you are getting healthier; (c) you are getting wealthier.

(6) Keep searching for every honest money-making opportunity you can find.

(7) Accept every chance to earn money—no matter how small the amount may be.

(8) Try to learn from every business deal—seek to learn at least one new fact about business and one new fact about people from every deal you're in.

(9) Keep learning no matter what your age, wealth, or health. An active mind makes for a healthier body.

(10) Remember that health is very much a matter of your state of mind—a constructive, positive outlook on wealth and your movement upward in the world can do much to improve your health.

(11) *Follow your doctor's orders in mind and action!*

Now here are some useful books on health that are well worth your attention. Try to read a few of these books during the next four weeks.

USEFUL BOOKS ON YOUR HEALTH

Alvarez—*Live at Peace with Your Nerves*, Prentice-Hall

Blanton and Gordon—*Now or Never: The Promise of the Middle Years*, Prentice-Hall

Cerney—*Stay Younger—Live Longer Through the Magic of Mental Self-Conditioning*, Parker Pub. Co.

Corbett—*Help Yourself to Better Sight*, Prentice-Hall

Cummings—*Stay Young and Vital*, Prentice-Hall

Devi—*Forever Young, Forever Healthy*, Prentice-Hall

Devi—*Renew Your Life Through Yoga*, Prentice-Hall

Dunne—*Yoga Made Easy*, Prentice-Hall

Hutschnecker—*The Will to Happiness*, Prentice-Hall

Hutschnecker—*The Will to Live*, Prentice-Hall

Kennedy—*Relax and Live*, Prentice-Hall

Neal—*God Can Heal You Now*, Prentice-Hall

Page—*How to Lick Executive Stress*, Prentice-Hall

Peale—*Inspiring Messages for Daily Living*, Prentice-Hall

Peale—*Stay Alive All Your Life*, Prentice-Hall

Petrie—*How to Reduce and Control Your Weight Through Self-Hypnotism*, Parker Pub. Co.

Petrie—*Martinis and Whipped Cream: The New Carbo-cal Way to Lose Weight and Stay Slim*, Parker Pub. Co.

Rawls—*Yoga for Beauty and Health*, Parker Pub. Co.

Robert—*The Cavett Robert Personal Development Course*, Parker Pub. Co.

Schindler—*How to Live 365 Days a Year*, Prentice-Hall

Wade—*Helping Yourself with Enzymes*, Parker Pub. Co.

Wade—*The Natural Laws of Healthful Living*, Parker Pub. Co.

Wallis—*Figure Improvement and Body Conditioning Through Exercise*, Prentice-Hall

Wilson—*Double Your Energy and Live Without Fatigue*, Prentice-Hall

four

Following Your
Stars to a
Great Fortune

There are millions of ways for you to become a millionaire. While we can't cover all of these ways in one book, we can suggest a number of them. And one of the ways to become a millionaire which seems to work well for many people is the ancient but rapidly growing *art of astrology*. Let's see why.

Use the Stars to Guide Your Fortune Hunting

Les C. is a great salesman, yet he never begins a sales trip or interview without first having consulted his astrological prediction or horoscope for that day. "I use my horoscope in either of two ways," Les says. "If my horoscope or prediction is positive, I use it to spur me on, to give myself additional confidence. But if the prediction for the day is negative, I use it in a positive way to alert myself to the dangers and problems I face. This keeps me on my toes at all times and helps me make more sales."

Les should know the value of astrology because he sells more than $2 million worth of specialty items a year, working out of his home. With a commission which averages 10 percent of his sales, Les earns more than $200,000 per year. "My only boss is my wife," Les laughs. "And I have her pretty well trained to leave me alone!"

Now I'm not saying that you must *believe* in astrology to be a top-level salesman. But I do say this:

Belief in a force external to yourself can provide enormous motivation and self-confidence which lead to great wealth.

Les uses the stars to guide his hunt for a fortune. You may want to consider doing the same. If you do, this chapter can get you started on your way to wealth through the stars.

What Astrology Does for People

Most people everywhere in this world seek strength and guidance from a power greater than themselves. Some people find the needed strength and guidance in prayer and religion. Others turn to astrology.

Astrology is *not* a religion, but it may serve some of the purposes of religion for certain people. So you need not give up your religion when you become interested in or use astrology.

Now what might astrology do for you? It might:

• Spur you on to greater wealth efforts
• Give you comfort when you're blue
• Guide your wealth efforts
• Chase away a feeling of emptiness you may now have
• Explain why your luck has been bad recently
• Make you feel more at home in the world

What Astrology Is

Most astrologists believe that the events in each of our lives can be determined from a study of certain stars and heavenly bodies. Knowing the date and time of your birth, either you or an astrologer can prepare an astrological forecast or horoscope of the future events in your life. Some astrologers will study 57 or more factors in your astrological sphere before preparing your horoscope.

Most astrological forecasts revolve around money, love, security, family, job, and related items. From *your* wealth standpoint you might use your horoscope or forecast to determine:

- Your lucky days
- Times for extreme caution
- Types of people to avoid
- Profitable businesses for you
- Lucrative deals you can make
- Parts of the world that may bring wealth to you

An interesting aspect of astrology is that:

A positive forecast or horoscope can spur you on to greater wealth efforts; a negative forecast can alert you to possible problems and help you avoid them.

Thus, your astrological horoscope or forecast can be useful and profitable—be it positive or negative.

Why Astrology May Help You

Wealth-builders and millionaires come in all sizes, shapes, and with varying backgrounds. Since I meet thousands of wealth-builders and a certain number of millionaires every year, I believe I know a little about both types of people. One fact I've noted about both is this:

Beginning wealth-builders and millionaires, alike, seek whatever outside stimulus they can find to spur them on in their wealth search.

Or if you have the motivation to build wealth but do not understand people, astrology may be your answer. Here, in concise form, is an astrological guide to people and their characteristics.

Analyze Business Associates with Astrology

If you use astrology to analyze a business associate, you may—if you know his birthday—be able to figure him out in advance. Try the following list on yourself, your relatives, and your business associates and see!

ASTROLOGICAL GUIDE TO PEOPLE

Birth Date	Astrological Character Traits
Dec. 22 to Jan. 19	Born under the sign of Capricornus, these people work hard, are thrifty, cautious, unloving, cold, slow, doleful, and pessimistic. They often hit it big in their own business.
Jan. 20 to Feb. 18	Born under the sign of Aquarius, these people love water sports, may be lazy, dissatisfied, pleasant, and friendly. They seldom lose their temper, and are usually quiet and peaceful. They may, however, delay things more than is good for themselves and others.
Feb. 19 to March 20	Born under the sign of Pisces, these people are loving, forthright, truthful, trustworthy, kind, generous, and lovers of beauty. They are easily directed or led.
March 21 to April 19	Born under the sign of Aries, these people are often business executives because they are driving and energetic. As leaders they may dream great dreams and be deep thinkers who want to act freely and do things their way. They may, at times, be obstinate.
April 20 to May 20	Born under the sign of Taurus, these people are strong in both mind and body, brave, gentle, kind, emotional, and understanding. They can, however, be troublesome and dangerous.

Birth Date	Astrological Character Traits
May 21 to June 20	Born under the sign of Gemini, these people are both thinkers and doers. They are kind, gentle, and extremely generous. Most of these people speak well and can communicate easily with others.
June 21 to July 22	Born under the sign of Cancer, these people are hard-driving, ambitious, dedicated, intuitive, enjoy travel, and are changeable in love affairs.
July 23 to Aug. 22	Born under the sign of Leo, these people are serious, polite, gentle, courageous, and understanding.
Aug. 23 to Sept. 22	Born under the sign of Virgo, these people are well organized, precise, and methodical. Attracted by the intelligence of others, they are proud, faithful, good students, and excellent business builders.
Sept. 23 to Oct. 22	Born under the sign of Libra, these people are cultured lovers of peace, may be spendthrifts, are often graceful in their walk, and gifted in speech and appearance.
Oct. 23 to Nov. 21	Born under the sign of Scorpio, these people are brave, well-spoken, ambitious, polite, and in complete charge of themselves.
Nov. 22 to Dec. 21	Born under the sign of Sagittarius, these people are emphatic, impulsive, self-confident, sports lovers, and somewhat impulsive.

There you have a quick rundown of what astrologers say about people born at different times of the year. So the next time you run into a tough business opponent:

• Find out the date of his birth

- Look up his traits in the above list
- Use this information to guide your actions

Surround Yourself with Money

Ben F. used the above list *after* he got started on his fortune building. Here's how.

Ben is a regular reader of the well-known and highly respected monthly newsletter *International Wealth Success*. This helpful publication shows wealth-builders how and where to get:

- 100% financing for real estate
- 100% financing for new factories
- 100% backing for compensating-balance loans
- Quick money for any business need
- World-wide business loans
- Loans for people with low credit ratings

Ben sent the above newsletter his annual subscription fee of $24.00 to P.O. Box 186, Merrick, N. Y. 11566. Within a few weeks his mind was full of new ideas for hitting the big money. "What I want to do is surround myself with money," Ben said. "The *International Wealth Success* newsletter showed me exactly how to do this. Then I used my horoscope to predict my good days and profitable business."

Sell—Borrow—Buy—Repay—Profit

"I was interested in export-import, and my horoscope showed that it would be profitable for me," Ben said. "The IWS newsletter gave me two or more pages a month of listings of overseas firms wanting to buy products from firms in the United States, serve as sales agents for various products manufactured here, or having items ready for import. Reading this excellent newsletter gave me some 60 or more profitable export-import leads every month. Of course, there were also hundreds of other leads covering quick financing, real estate, finder's opportunities, mail order, etc.

"But one big point I didn't realize—until the newsletter pointed it out—was this:

> "Overseas firms will often pay you in advance for U.S. products you have located for them. This means the only capital you need is for stamps and envelopes—less than $10."

So here's what Ben did. He used his *International Wealth Success* newsletter and a copy of their book *Worldwide Riches Opportunities* to:

- Locate overseas firms seeking U.S. products
- Sell them the products they need
- Borrow, on the basis of the purchase order, enough to cover the purchase
- Buy the items ordered using the loan
- Ship the items ordered
- Repay the borrowed money using the income from the sale
- Bank the profit

Ben's eyes were really opened and he shook with glee when he discovered that the loans obtained this way were:

- Low interest
- Easy to obtain
- Never involved credit investigation
- Obtainable from many firms at the same time
- Fast and certain

Thus, Ben was "doing business on air" because he never really had to put up any money except for postage and envelopes.

Collect from Your Sellers

Another source of income Ben discovered was the commission he could earn on the sale of the products to his overseas customers. Thus, the company for which Ben sold the items would pay him a five or ten percent commission for making the sale. Further, Ben collected a profit on each sale to his overseas customers. This agreed with his horoscope which predicted that Ben would earn money from many people throughout the world.

Ben's first overseas customers were firms seeking astrological products including:

- Books and diaries
- Horoscope wheels
- Maps of the heavens
- Statues and pictures

Within a year after starting his export-import business Ben was earning $110,000 per year. Today, a few years later, Ben's income is in the $200,000-per-year range.

Put Your Horoscope to Work

Your horoscope predicts your future for a day, a month, a year, or longer. You can put your horoscope to work if you believe in astrology.

That's exactly what Clyde K. did when his horoscope, which was prepared by an astrologer read: *You will find great success among large crowds of people.* And: *Help others and you will help yourself.* Here's what Clyde K. did to put his horoscope to work:

(1) Searched for a way to help others.
(2) Found a good idea.
(3) Invested $235 in his idea.
(4) Put his idea into action.
(5) Collected $1,827 income in three days.
(6) Earns $92,000 per year in his spare time.

Now let's examine Clyde's success somewhat more closely. This is what he did. He:

(A) Searched for a way to combine crowds of people with helping them for a profit.
(B) Came on the idea of giving weekend parties for lonely people.
(C) Rented an apartment in a nice neighborhood.
(D) Advertised pleasant, no-alcohol parties for three age groups (18–24 yrs), (25–35 yrs), (36 and over), for Friday, Saturday, and Sunday evenings.
(E) Charged an admission fee of $3 per person.
(F) Used an old hi-fi and some cast-off furniture to decorate the apartment.

(G) Had these attendance figures the first three evenings: 210; 218; 198 persons.

Today Clyde runs these same parties three nights a week—year-round. His spare-time income from the parties now exceeds $90,000 per year. That's not bad for a man who drives a bus as his regular job.

Remember this about your horoscope or any other prediction of your future:

> If you believe in what you're trying to do, it will be much easier to reach your goal.

So while I'm not saying that astrology will bring you wealth, I am saying that:

- Belief builds wealth
- Positive beliefs are good for you
- Action-producing beliefs are beneficial
- Lack of belief can cause failure

Make Astrology Work for You

Astrology is an interesting topic to most people—even to those who scoff at it. Why is this so? Because:

- Everyone is interested in himself
- Astrology tells us about ourselves
- There is a degree of truth in every horoscope
- People recognize this truth and are intrigued

Thus, you need not be a complete believer in astrology to make it work for you by:

(1) Using the facts in your horoscope, or
(2) Preparing, and selling, astrological products, or
(3) Opening, and running, an astrological business, or
(4) Becoming an astrological consultant

If you are a firm believer in astrology, please don't be shocked by my suggesting that semi-believers put astrology to work for themselves. Why? I have observed throughout the world that:

People believe in that which gives them results. If they are doubters at the start, they are soon converted to believers by positive results.

Today astrology is big business everywhere. And every day of the week more people are taking up the study of astrology. Look around you to see the evidences of the popularity of astrology as shown by:

- Daily newspaper columns (a total of 1,200 in the U.S.)
- Numerous magazines
- Hundreds of books
- Clubs and organizations
- Computer preparation of horoscopes
- Dating services
- Cookbooks based on astrology
- Astrological marriage guides
- Horoscopic records and tapes

How might you enter astrology as a business? There are many different ways. You might:

- Prepare horoscopes for individuals
- Write a column or book
- Develop new astrological devices for sale
- Advise newcomers to the field

Thus, you can make a profitable part-time or full-time business of astrology. You may even find that your belief in astrology will grow with your success!

Consider Becoming an Astrologer

Let's explore, a little further, the idea of making astrology work for you. Almost every astrologer in business today (some 5,000 in the U.S.) is self-trained. Why? Because there are few formal training courses. Yet astrology is an ancient art. Some of the oldest recorded writings of man are astrological notations on tablets dating back to 3,000 B.C.

If you do become an astrologer, what can you do with your knowledge? You can:

- Consult for companies. (Numerous firms now use an astrologer to guide future business actions.)
- Prepare horoscopes for businessmen. (J. P. Morgan built a fortune and is said to have regularly consulted an astrologer.)
- Cast you own business horoscope. (Yes, astrology is a do-it-yourself activity which can help you earn more money.)
- Help others by preparing their business and personal horoscopes to guide their future activities.

How can you sell your astrological services? There are numerous ways, including:

- Mail order (you advertise in the astrology magazines)
- Personal interviews with clients
- Computer printout of the horoscope for sale in stores

In suggesting that you consider becoming an astrologer I have four ideas in mind:

(1) The knowledge you gain may give you an added interest in life.
(2) You may be able to earn a big income using your knowledge.
(3) Preparing your own horoscope can help you understand yourself.
(4) Your horoscope may lead you to greater financial success.

Though many people scoff at astrology, no one has yet proven that astrology is *bad* for people. In fact, studies by psychologists and psychiatrists show that the usual horoscope makes positive recommendations for people. Thus, in considering the possibility of studying astrology you are doing something positive and beneficial for yourself.

Combine Astrology with Self-Confidence

In chapter one we show you ways to increase your self-confidence while building your fortune. If the facts and evidence presented there are not sufficiently strong to motivate you, try combining astrology with building up your self-confidence. The combination can pack more power than the newest rocket blasting off to outer space.

How can you combine astrology and self-confidence? Here's your answer.

(1) Obtain your horoscope—either from an astrologer or by preparing it yourself.
(2) Underline the positive predictions given in your horoscope.
(3) Convince yourself that these positive predictions *can* come true.
(4) Work at making the predictions which you can control come true.
(5) As each prediction comes true, check it off on your horoscope.
(6) Feel your self-confidence rise as you make each controllable prediction come true.

Ron K. combined astrology and self-confidence in a grand attempt to get rich within one year after starting his business activities. Did he reach his goal, you ask? Yes; he not only reached his money goal—he went way beyond it. In fact, Ron K. hit his money goal within eight months after he started his program. Here's how he did it.

Get Rich Fast Using Your Horoscope

Ron prepared his own horoscope for the coming year. Then he took action to:

(a) List all the positive money forecasts; there were three:
   1. March is a good month to start a business
   2. You can be a star salesman
   3. People will listen if you speak loudly
(b) Devise a way to combine the three forecasts:
   1. He reviewed his likes and dislikes
   2. Decided to do what he liked best

3. Chose mail-order sales as his business
(c) Borrow money to start his mail-order business:
   1. He bought a copy of *Business Capital Sources* *
   2. Studied the hundreds of capital sources listed
   3. Applied for his loan
   4. Obtained the money quickly and easily
(d) Start his business:
   1. Chose his product using the forecasts
   2. Used the newsletter *International Wealth Success* as a source of money ideas
   3. Sold his product widely

"This all sounds great," you say. "But what did he sell and how did he make the big money? Also, how much did Ron *really* make in his first year?"

These are all excellent questions and I'm delighted you asked them. They show that you're thinking along the right lines to make big money yourself. Now here are your answers.

Ron combined the three predictions by starting his business in March, speaking loudly so people would listen, and becoming a star salesman.

Seek, and Do, the Unusual

Ron wanted to go into mail order. But at the same time he wanted to be a star salesman and to speak loudly so people would listen to him. His problem, then, was how to combine the mail order and loud talk. Ron soon realized that any answer that was to fill his needs had to be unusual.

Studying mail-order procedures, Ron noticed that much attention was given to the covering letter, how it was worded, and what it said. Then a great thought came to him:

(1) Why not *talk* my letter?
(2) Send a small record instead of a letter.
(3) The unusual might make big sales.

---

* *Business Capital Sources* lists hundreds and hundreds of money sources. Available for $15 from IWS Inc., P.O. Box 186, Merrick, N.Y. 11566.

Be Sure of Your Facts

Ron immediately went to his local public library to do some quick research. He investigated the:

- Number of record players in the U.S. and the world
- Incomes of homes owning record players
- Number of tape recorders and players in the U.S. and the world
- Incomes of homes owning tape players
- Cost of making recordings

With these facts in hand, Ron immediately felt more self-confident. Why? Because he:

(1) Developed an unusual solution to his problem.
(2) Investigated a situation on his own and came up with the facts.
(3) Was ready to move ahead on his own.
(4) Discovered he could send a recorded message for less than a regular letter.
(5) Had broken through a thinking barrier.

This brings us to the important concept that says:

Self-confidence springs from within when you use your mind to develop the new or unusual.

Test Your Ideas

Ron made a test mailing of his recorded sales message to 100 homes owning record players. To prevent a misleading result, Ron offered books for sale instead of products related to the record player. The response was enormous.

Next he offered records, albums, needles, cleaners, etc. This time the response was even greater.

Today Ron is selling some $3 million per year in mail-order products to both record and tape player owners using his recorded sales message. With a profit of 12% before taxes, Ron's net is

$360,000 per year—not bad for a man who combined astrology with self-confidence to come up with a winner!

Work Other Combinations

You can also combine astrology with mind power and health improvement. The process is simple. All you do is:

(1) Prepare, or obtain, your horoscope for the current year.
(2) Study the business predictions carefully.
(3) Relate, where possible, the business predictions to mind power or health.
(4) Develop an income-producing job or business around the predictions.
(5) Go on to great success and a fortune.

You can also combine astrology with many of the other topics in this book. We will point this out as we go along.

Once again, astrology may be able to bring riches to you, even though you may be a disbeliever. Try it today to see if it is the answer you need. Remember—you have nothing to lose because the time you devote to astrology will be repaid with increased knowledge or, possibly, great wealth. So get started today!

USEFUL BOOKS ON ASTROLOGY

Now here are a number of useful books on astrology which you'll find interesting and helpful. Try to read as many of these as you can.

American Federation of Astrologers—*Basic Principles of Astrology*, Llewellyn Publications.
Ayer, V. A.—*Everyday Astrology*, Tudor Publishing Co.
Ballantyne, N.—*Your Horoscope and Your Dreams*, Franconia Publishing Co.
Carter, C. E.—*Principles of Astrology*, The Theosophical Publishing House.
Day, H.—*Seeing into the Future*, Borden Publishing Co.
Fairfax, F.—*Key to Astrology*, Wehman Brothers.

Gauguelin, M.—*Cosmic Clocks: The Scientific Implications of Astrology*, Henry Regnery Co.

George, L.—*A to Z Horoscope Maker and Delineator*, Llewellyn Publications.

Goodavage, J. F.—*Astrology: The Space-Age Science*, Prentice-Hall, Inc.

Heindel, M.—*Simplified Scientific Astrology*, Rosicrucian Fellowship.

Jones, H. E.—*How to Learn Astrology*, Llewellyn Publications.

Lyndoe, E.—*Astrology for Everyone*, E. P. Dutton & Co.

Marsden, J.—*Follow Your Stars to Success*, Llewellyn Publications.

Mayo, J.—*How to Cast a Natal Chart*, S. Weiser.

Scott, J.—*Celestial Scene: A Horoscope Guide to Turn You On*, Grossett & Dunlap, Inc.

Vorel, I.—*Be Your Own Astrologer*, Wehman Brothers.

five

How to Develop
a Rich
Mental Attitude

Believe it or not *what* you think, and the *way* you think, can make you rich! And, as everyone knows, the power to think is completely free and available to all of us. To think you don't need a:

- Factory
- Payroll
- Bank account
- Lawyer

or any of the other trappings that go with a business. But to *use* thinking to make ourselves rich we must *direct* our thoughts.

Control Your Thoughts

If you were to ask me the two extremes of human thinking with respect to wealth and money, I'd answer you thus:

- You can have a *rich mental attitude*, i.e., a *positive extreme*, or

- You can have a *poor mental attitude,* i.e., a *negative extreme*

And, surprising as it may seem, the difference between two people, one of whom has hit it *big* and the other who is still struggling to make his first $1,000, is that the man who made it big has a *rich mental attitude.* He is what I call the *positive extreme,* while the man who hasn't made it is the *negative extreme.*

What Is a Rich Mental Attitude?

A rich mental attitude is a state of mind in which you:

Look at the positive aspects of every money and business situation so that you understand it better, take action when action is needed, and strive for the best from yourself and from others.

Thus, a Rich Mental Attitude (RMA) helps you to:

- Understand
- Act
- Obtain

When you *understand* the importance of every money situation that occurs in your business you are in a more favorable position than when you lack understanding or comprehension. With understanding you can *act.* And as we all know, life is empty without action because action enables us to obtain what we seek.

So to adopt a Rich Mental Attitude you should:

- Seek the positive aspects of every money and business situation
- Try to understand every such situation
- Take action whenever necessary
- Strive for the best from yourself and others

What an RMA Does for You

Adopt a Rich Mental Attitude and money miracles begin to occur in your life.

You find, after a few days, that:

- You are beginning to live better
- Your knowledge of business is wider
- You get more done in less time
- You now *act* instead of just dreaming

Paddy L. adopted an RMA and became so wealthy so fast that it almost frightened him. "I never realized the enormous role that thinking plays in making us rich," Paddy says, "For years I was poor; today I'm richer than I ever dreamed I would or could be. And it all came from my RMA."

Here's how Paddy L. hit the big money in a few months—starting with hardly any capital at all. Paddy L.:

(1) *Decided*—as an experiment which wouldn't cost him a penny—to adopt a Rich Mental Attitude.
(2) *Listed* his assets and debts and found—like many other people—that he owed more than he owned.
(3) *Concluded* that he had to increase his income and his assets—i.e., what was coming in and what he owned.

Once having made these decisions Paddy L. was ready to take action to put his RMA to work. Now let's see how Paddy L. converted his RMA to *big* money.

Turn Your RMA Into *Big* Money

Paddy L. had some problems in his life which I've found many other people—particularly beginning wealth-builders—also have. Paddy's major problems were:

- Money shortage—Paddy was so low on cash that his wallet was as thin as a dollar bill.
- Poor credit rating—Paddy hadn't taken the time or effort to establish his borrowing power.
- Few friends with money—Most of Paddy's friends were poorer than he. Hence, they weren't of much help when it came to lending him money or becoming a cosigner on a loan.
- Idea shortage—Paddy didn't have too many ideas on how to convert his RMA to *big* money.

Thinking about these problems, Paddy came to the conclusion that what he had to do was:

(1) Develop a source of income for himself which would bring *capital* to him.

(2) Invest this capital which other people put in his hands so it earned an income *both* for himself and the people placing the capital with him.

(3) Continue building both his own income and that of his backers using his ingenuity and knowledge of a profitable business field.

Get Rich in Less Than One Year

Once he had these ideas, Paddy L. combined them with his RMA by beginning his search for wealth. One day, while reading the newspaper, Paddy saw a news item which stated that sheets or blocks of modern American and British stamps rose rapidly in value—by as much as two thirds of their value per year—when held by investors. This meant, according to Paddy's calculations, that $1.00 invested in sheets or blocks of stamps on January 1 would be worth $1.66 on December 31 of the same year. It was just the idea Paddy L. was looking for. Taking this idea, Paddy:

(1) Checked out those U.S. and foreign stamp sheets having the greatest rise in value in recent years.

(2) Decided that he would form a stamp investment firm that would invest funds for people in stamp sheets of either his choice or the investor's choice. Paddy visualized himself as a "stamp stock broker"—that is, he would invest other people's money in stamps instead of stocks.

(3) Wrote for publication a letter to the editor of each stamp magazine published in the U.S. and Britain describing his planned stamp investment service (this free publicity cost only the time, paper, and postage involved—a total of less than $50).

(4) Waited for responses from the readers of the letters after they were published in the various stamp magazines.

(5) Began collecting money hand over fist.

"But what was Paddy's idea?" you ask. "I still don't know what put those bundles of money into his hands." All right, here are the details of Paddy's *big money* idea.

Think Rich and Be Rich

As soon as Paddy read of the growth in the value of stamp sheets and blocks which were held for one year or more, he decided to become a manager of stamp investments for people interested in investing in stamps. You don't need a license or any special qualifications to do this. You just open your business and start collecting the money. Here's how Paddy did it—you can easily do the same.

(1) Formed his business by choosing a suitable name and by having 100 letterheads printed.

(2) Registered his business with the local county clerk.

(3) Selected his stamp investment units—i.e., the smallest sum he would accept from his customers—as a start he chose $500.

(4) Wrote the letters to the editors of the stamp magazines, as mentioned above. (Note that many magazines publish letters to the editor quickly and at no cost to the writer of the letter.)

(5) Set up a simple filing system using cardboard boxes which recorded the money he received.

(6) Invested the money he received in stamp sheets and blocks after deducting a suitable (10%) investment fee.

(7) Informed his clients by mail every two months of the current value of their stamp portfolio.

During his first year in business, Paddy received $500 each from more than two thousand people. His total capital in-flow was thus: 2,080 people ($500 per person) = $1,040,000. With a fee of 10%, Paddy's income for the first year was $104,000. Since he invested some of this in stamps himself, Paddy's capital grew and he profited in the same way his clients did.

Seek the Simple, Big Money Business

Paddy's business has several highly desirable features. These are:

(1) It is simple—he deals only in money and thin postage stamps.
(2) Each sale is a *big* sale—i.e., $500 or more.
(3) Paddy receives his commission (almost all of which is profit) immediately.
(4) The revenue potential is large—by this I mean Paddy doesn't work all year for a measly $25,000 or $30,000.
(5) There is an enormous growth potential in Paddy's business—as more people become interested in stamps the market for his investment service grows.
(6) As tax rates on ordinary income rise, people become more interested in capital-gain opportunities, which increases the number of Paddy's potential customers, because their profits from his service are capital gains.
(7) Paddy's business is basically a mail-order business.

Develop Your New Way of Life Using RMA

Paddy's million-dollar-per-year business resulted from his adopting an RMA—*Rich Mental Attitude*. You can adopt *your* RMA this instant. It won't cost you a penny to do so and it may make you a fortune. Also, you can take Paddy's basic idea of a simple, big-money business and adopt it to *your* way of life. Let's see how.

(1) Seek a new way to solve an old problem. (Paddy found a *new* way to earn capital gains for his clients.)
(2) Devise a low-cost way to promote your idea. (Paddy wrote letters to the editors of magazines; later he advertised in the classified columns of the same magazines.)
(3) Arrange to take an immediate profit for yourself. (Paddy takes his 10% commission.)
(4) Avoid (at the beginning, at least) any business requiring a license or other highly specialized training.

(5) Don't deal in perishable products (foods, flowers, etc.) or in medicines if you plan to promote your items by mail order.

(6) Promote—if you can—by mail order instead of direct sales using salesmen.

(7) Set a sales target for yourself and work hard to achieve your goal. Don't give up until you reach your goal.

(8) Keep improving your basic idea each time you make a sale. Try to learn something useful for your business from each sale you make.

(9) Be an idea man or woman—that is seek out business ideas everywhere. One good idea, such as Paddy's can make you rich forever.

(10) Cultivate at all times your RMA—think rich, look rich, act rich, and you'll be rich!

(11) Make your RMA *your new way of life*.

Put Other People's Money to Work for You

One aspect of an RMA that many people fail to see is this:

Your RMA is a money magnet. People with money will seek you out to *ask* you to borrow money from them so you can put it to work earning a return for both themselves and yourself.

Just imagine if you could buy a money magnet how much you'd be willing to pay for it! Your RMA *is* a powerful magic mind secret and an enormous money magnet which can attract huge sums of cash into your waiting hands.

Mike D. found his RMA such a powerful magic money magnet to rich people who wanted him to invest their money that he had to:

(1) Change his home phone number to an unlisted number.

(2) Use a post office box number for his business address.

(3) Alter his style of clothing so people wouldn't recognize him too readily.

(4) Go to a new summer resort area where he wasn't known.

(5) Learn how to confuse people who were following or "tailing" him.

(6) Acquire the skills of a private detective to protect himself from people wanting to throw money in his face for him to invest.

How did Mike D. generate so much enthusiasm amongst people with money? That's easy to answer. Mike analyzed himself and his friends, after deciding to adopt a Rich Mental Attitude. Here's what Mike learned about himself and his friends:

* Most people are perpetually short of cash
* People with fabulous business ideas are so strapped for cash they can hardly ever put their ideas to work
* Most people are afraid of loan companies, banks, and other "marble-hall" type lending agencies
* The fear people have of banks and loan organizations just makes it more difficult for them to borrow money when they need it

Recognizing these facts, Mike decided to become a "poor man's financial broker, finder, business broker, and consultant." Mike sent $99.50 to IWS, Inc., P.O. Box 186, Merrick, N.Y. 11566, for their easy-to-use *Financial Broker-Finder-Business Broker-Consultant Program*. Within a few weeks Mike was amazed to realize that this excellent program had shown him:

(1) *Where* he could borrow millions of dollars.
(2) *How* he could set himself up in business.
(3) *Who* his customers might be.
(4) *When* to start his business (*Now!*).
(5) *What* his clients might need.
(6) *Why* he should start now.

Dream Yourself to Riches

So Mike D. became a financial broker and business consultant. Why? Because Mike loves people and he gets enormous pleasure out of helping little people. What background in business did Mike have? He had some business experience and he studied his program and numerous business books carefully. Whom did Mike help? Here are thumbnail details. Mike decided to:

(1) Help small business people.
(2) Concentrate in his local area.
(3) Charge low fees.
(4) Put wealthy people's money to work.

To start, Mike sent business announcement notices to his local papers and magazines, using the forms provided in his program. The notice told people that he was opening a financial broker business. He also applied the other publicity recommendations given in his program.

Within a few days Mike had more than 100 wealthy people banging on his door, pleading with him to:

• Take their money and invest it in a safe, growing business
• Manage their profits from these safe, growing businesses

Thus, Mike had dreamed himself into great wealth. Why? Because:

(1) He has an enormous supply of money readily available at:
    (a) No cost
    (b) Without investigation
    (c) Free of credit checks
    (d) Clear of job history checks
    (e) Without pleading with bank vice presidents
(2) He has an infinite number of places to put the money to work because:
    (a) People *come* to him for money
    (b) He can choose to make the best loans
    (c) He collects a commission on all loans he places
    (d) He charges *both* the lender *and* borrower a commission
    (e) His RMA is always with him

Feel Good—Help Others

Mike D. helps the small, the needy, the poor, the ambitious, the hard-working people of the world. "This makes me feel great," Mike says. "There's nothing as stimulating as helping someone because *it enables them to help others too.* Thus, you spread goodness, and wealth, everywhere."

Who did, and does, Mike help? Here's a quick list of just a few to whom Mike made, and makes, loans:

- Local housewife who developed a special grass seed and unique type of rose in her basement. Loan $10,000. Business volume two years later $185,000 per year. Profits enormous.
- Home woodcarving hobbyist who spent most of his evenings at home carving interesting items in his workshop; also taught youngsters how to work with wood. A $25,000 loan enabled this hobbyist to open both a store featuring wood carvings *and* a school for training people interested in the hobby. Profit the first year after the loan was $78,000.
- Pet lover converted knowledge of special toys for dogs and cats into a thriving mail-order business, starting with a $5,000 loan. The loan paid for the first few advertising mailings and the inventory for the orders. Income two years after the start $167,000 per year. Profits delightful.
- Construction school for cost estimating and profit control was started by a carpenter in his spare time using a $3,000 loan. Today he has schools in three states and gives many other courses. Annual net profit is $56,000, and growing rapidly.
- Real-estate operator borrowed $30,000 to buy several apartment houses. Today his expanded real-estate empire nets him over $125,000 per year tax-free because of the large depreciation allowances.
- Golfer became a golf cart dealer using a $10,000 loan. Today he also sells small electric and gasoline-powered carts and vehicles. Income now exceeds $200,000 per year.

Back an Idea Using Your RMA

In each of the six successes above Mike D. backed an *idea,* using his Rich Mental Attitude (RMA). He certainly hoped in each case that the idea would turn into a profit. But it was the *idea,* and the person behind it, which first led Mike to consider backing it. And even though Mike was using Other People's Money (OPM) to back Other People's Ideas (OPI), he acted as though it was his own money he was investing. This leads us to an important concept, namely:

> To judge the commercial worth of one of your ideas, ask yourself: If I had $10,000 which I saved from my earlier earnings would I invest it in this idea?

If your answer is Yes, then go ahead and invest. But if your answer is No, turn away from the idea for awhile. Put it on the "back burner" as people say. That is:

> Never give up on good ideas. Just delay investing in what appear to be good ideas until your answer to the question of investing is Yes.

Go the Public Route with RMA

The United States is the greatest country in the world. Those of you who've read my other money books know that I travel all over the world on business. For example, this chapter is being written in a hotel room in Rome, Italy, close by Vatican City. I'm in Rome for some important business deals. At the moment I'm waiting for a man who wants to borrow $100,000 from me.

In traveling the world over on business, one gets to see and understand a little about other countries. While I have the greatest respect for people everywhere, I still believe that the United States is the greatest country in the world. Why? Because in the United States:

People have a strong success drive—they are willing to take a risk to make their dreams come true. This willingness to take a risk can tie in beautifully with your RMA.

The best example of risk taking in the United States is our stock market. In the stock market people risk their money by investing in other people's businesses. If you take the IWS Financial Broker-Finder-Business Broker-Consultant Program, as Mike D. did, you'll get all the information you need to take any company—yours or someone else's—public in the stock market. By a public sale I mean that you can arrange to sell stock to the public and obtain anywhere from $1,000 to $10,000,000, or more, for the company you represent, or for your own company. For your company you can use this money to pay:

- Your salary
- Travel and entertainment costs
- Purchase costs of machinery, autos, etc.
- Price of buildings, land, etc.

Thus, you can use the proceeds from a public stock offering to pay any legitimate corporate expense.

"But what has a public stock offering got to do with RMA?" you ask. Just this:

When you have an RMA, it shows through in your stock offering data—people become enthused about buying the stock in your company.

And there are plenty of people in the United States—and the rest of the world for that matter—who are ready to buy your stock when you go public. Why? Because when you have a Rich Mental Attitude people are ready to invest in *you!*

How the Public Can Help You

Mike D., using the complete instructions covering the selling of all kinds of stock to the public in his Financial Broker-Finder-Business Broker-Consultant Program, was able to obtain from the public for his clients:

$300,000 for a mail-order operator
$1,000,000 for a real-estate syndicate

$200,000 for a home hobbyist
$500,000 for a specialty manufacturer
$400,000 for himself in his financial-finder business

Now I'd like to tell you what happened to just three of the stocks which Mike D. took public. Here are the facts:

Stock A: Offered first at 50¢ per share; two years later the stock was selling for $68 per share.

Stock B: Sold for $1 per share for a company which hadn't yet earned a penny, the stock was worth $30 per share two years later.

Stock C: First offered at $20 per share and sold out, the stock rose to $112 per share, split two-for-one and today is worth $90 per share.

I could give you at least fifty similar cases where small, struggling, capital-short firms went public and wound up with a pot of gold. Why is a public stock offering linked with your RMA so important to you? Because:

(1) You don't have to repay the money you obtain from the sale of your stock.
(2) There are no interest payments on the money.
(3) You can obtain as much money as you need—from $1,000 to $100,000,000, or more.
(4) If you need more money, you can always go back to the public and sell additional shares.

For full details on the step-by-step procedures for making a public stock offering, read the monthly newsletter *International Wealth Success*, and study their Financial Broker-Finder-Business Broker-Consultant Program. The newsletter subscription price is $24 per year, while the program is priced at $99.50. Both are available from IWS Inc., Box 186, Merrick, New York 11566, and they are well worth their price.

You Can't Miss with a Strong RMA

When you read one of my books I can't guarantee what results you'll achieve. But I can tell you this:

Develop a strong and hardy Rich Mental Attitude and you're bound to profit in many different ways because you'll attract, and do, good for others and for yourself.

Your RMA costs you nothing. All you need do is resolve—here and now—that you will:

- Live better
- Eat more nourishing food
- Own a more expensive car
- Take longer vacations
- Wear smarter clothes
- Live in a better house
- Seek a richer neighborhood
- Go out for fun more often
- Become a *big* success in life

Adopt *your* RMA today and a miracle will come into your life without costing you a cent. Truly, an RMA is one of the most powerful magic mind secrets ever invented to build enormous wealth.

For Positive Results, Hook Speed to RMA

As many of my readers know, I believe in speedy wealth building. Why sit for 30 years trying to get into the big money when you might be able to do the same in 3 years, which is only days in comparison to 30 years!

Now I fully recognize that there are limitations to speedy wealth building. For instance:

(1) Contracts take time.
(2) Investigations may be lengthy.
(3) Finance money may be slow in coming.

And so on. But—and I speak from long practical experience—it is possible to accelerate enormously your wealth accumulation. How? That's easy. *Hook speed to RMA and do as I say!*

In my lectures on business and wealth throughout the world I often meet doubting Thomases—those people who doubt everything anyone ever says. For years I wrestled with the problem of convincing these doubters that they should stop doubting and believe me. About six years ago I discovered the key thought for convincing these doubters. What I say to them is this:

> Ladies and gentlemen, I have nothing to sell you except *your* success. I have no patent medicines, muscle builders, youth tonics, or memory pills. What I do have though, are a number of explosively superb wealth-building ideas for you which are:
> - Proven
> - Practical
> - Profitable

Likewise, the idea of hooking speed to RMA to build gigantic riches quickly is *proven, practical,* and *profitable.* You can use a high-speed positive approach to wealth building with your Rich Mental Attitude without spending a cent. To prove this today, try the eight steps given below and watch your riches grow and grow!

(1) Look for the quick-turnover business, one in which you buy items today and sell them tomorrow.

(2) Avoid long contract negotiations, complicated title searches, and similar delays. (Why waste time and money sitting on your hands waiting for a deal to develop?)

(3) Seek the simple business, the business that requires the minimum labor, machinery, real estate, materials, etc.

(4) Accept a few dollars less profit in a simple business —the headaches you avoid make the smaller profit much more enjoyable!

(5) Keep several fast deals going at the same time— then if one fails you still have the others going.

(6) Weigh speed vs. delays in every new deal. If you accept a slow deal, be sure the reason is exceptionally high profits.

(7) Be businesslike at all times—seek the facts; don't allow your emotions to take over.

(8) Set and adhere to time goals for each new project. Make your fortune your destiny!

six

Making Your
Ambitions Pay Off
in Big Money

You have a river of pure gold in your mind! To turn this river of gold so it flows towards you and into your pockets, all you need do is make your ambitions pay off in big money. In this chapter we show you how to do exactly that.

Convert Ambitions to Actions

Ambitions like dreams are a beginning. Without ambitions or dreams we have little to motivate ourselves to build enormous wealth.

But ambitions and dreams have little power without *action*. Why? Because:

Action translates mental images, such as ambitions and dreams, into positive results—for example, a profitable business, a patentable idea, the sale of a new product or service.

We need ambitions to get us started toward taking action. But we have to convert our ambitions into actions if we are to move from a condition of a shortage of funds to a condition of having more money than we know how to spend. To combine the two words, Ambitions and Actions, remember that they both begin with the letter "A."

Why Your Actions Are Important

Actions prove, or disprove, your beliefs, ambitions, ideas. For years I've watched as people tittered or snarled when I mentioned the importance of:

(1) Keeping busy
(2) Earning more money
(3) Helping those in need
(4) Spreading goodness through the world
(5) Being friendly

Yet almost every one of those who scoffed at these ideas later came back to me and said: "Ty, I laughed and thought you were crazy when you said those things. But when I finally took some action and did what you said I should, I found out that those ideas are really true!"

Certainly they're true. *I have nothing to sell you except your success!* And, as you know, nothing succeeds like success.

So your actions are important because they allow you to prove, or disprove, your beliefs. *Without* action you're still in a land of dreams. *With* action, you're on your way to great wealth and immense happiness.

Know How Your Mind Works

For most people, the sequence of wealth actions is:

(1) Vague desire for more money
(2) Decision to search for income sources
(3) Conduct some research on possible income sources
(4) Loses interest
(5) Gets sudden idea for a money source

(6) Toys with the idea
(7) Drops idea

OR

(1) Takes action on idea
(2) Improves idea, as needed
(3) Earns big money from the idea

Review, for a moment, your own experience with money ideas in the past. Doesn't your experience agree—in the main—with the above list?

And won't you agree with the Beginning Wealth-Builder (BWB) who finds that:

The big problem in earning a fortune is in taking action —ideas are fairly easy to get—the hard part of making your fortune is putting ideas into action!

Since I'm human, just like you, I face the same problems you do. That's why, in this chapter I'm going to give you a diamond-studded solid-gold technique for *taking action and getting results* in your wealth-building efforts. This technique is so powerful that I *guarantee* that you'll obtain positive results from it if you apply the method properly. I call this technique *Self-Motivation Unlimited—SMU.*

Put Self-Motivation Into Your Wealth Search

To show you *how, when,* and *why* SMU can work in your life, I want to tell you about the most successful wealth-builder I know. His name is Kent C. and he's worth $300 million, which is a rather large fortune. Yet Kent built his first $100 million nest egg in just six years using Self-Motivation Unlimited. His next $200 million took only three years because he had the capital and experience from his first $100 million.

To start our short summary of Kent's use of SMU, I'd like to say that at age 45 Kent was broke, unemployed, divorced, sick, unlucky, and miserably depressed. Today, at age 54, Kent is:

- A millionaire three-hundred times over
- Busier than any other man in his city
- Married to a beautiful, charming girl

- Vibrantly healthy
- Full of enormous luck
- Ecstatically happy and elated

How could any person change so much in nine years, you ask? That's easy—he used Self-Motivation Unlimited. It didn't cost him a cent to use SMU—only time. Yet he turned his time investment into $300 million. You can do the same! Here's how.

Understand Self-Motivation Unlimited

Self-Motivation Unlimited (SMU) is a powerful money-generating technique which uses Auto-Hypnosis to create an enormous money and success drive in anyone interested in hitting a million-dollar bonanza. To use Auto-Hypnosis (also called Self-Hypnosis) to build your SMU, take these steps:

(1) Learn to *relax* completely
(2) When you're completely relaxed, *suggest* success ideas to yourself
(3) While you're relaxed, *analyze* what you can do to make the *big money*
(4) Also, while you're relaxed, figure out ways to *improve* your performance

Seven Questions to Tell You as It Is

Many people question the effectiveness of SMU. I try to answer their questions as frankly and as directly as possible. Since I think I know what *your* questions might be, I've included a number of them here. I hope they help you understand SMU and Auto-Hypnosis better. Here are the questions and their answers.

Q. Does Self-Motivation Unlimited have any relation to mysticism or magic?
  A. No—none at all. But let me tell you this. Some of the astounding results of SMU seem almost magical to some people! And why not? Wouldn't you see some magic in a system that put one million dollars in your pocket in a year, or less?

Q. Can Auto-Hypnosis injure me, make me do something wrong, or affect my mind?

    A. No! Never! Under Auto-Hypnosis you:

        (a) Will *never* injure yourself

        (b) Will *never* do anything *wrong*

        (c) Will *never* degrade your mind

              BUT YOU

        (d) Will *gain* stupendous money power

        (e) Will *accomplish* more, *sooner*

        (f) Will *expand* your innate abilities

        (g) Can become *very rich*, very soon

        (h) Can mine the *full depths* of your personality

Q. How does Auto-Hypnosis work?

    A. In a very simple manner. You just:

        (1) Relax

        (2) Rid yourself of irrelevant thoughts

        (3) Feed positive thoughts to your subconscious mind

        (4) Return to work highly motivated and success-oriented

Q. Why does Auto-Hypnosis work?

    A. Because you use one of your strongest allies—your subconscious mind—to help you achieve success.

Q. Can I use Auto-Hypnosis for other purposes?

    A. Certainly—and many people do. For example, people use this technique to:

        (a) Relieve persistent pain

        (b) Overcome personality faults

        (c) Change their attitude toward life

        (d) Rid themselves of the need for tranquilizers

        (e) Lose weight

        (f) Improve leisure skills—such as golf, bridge, tennis

However, we'll concentrate on your fortune skills in this book. But at the end of this chapter we list other books on Auto-Hypnosis which will help you use this technique for some, or all, of the purposes listed above.

Q. Do people ever use Auto-Hypnosis without knowing that they are doing so?

    A. Sure—you've probably used Auto-Hypnosis a number of times in your life without knowing you did.

Q. How, and when, might I have used Auto-Hypnosis without knowing it?

A. You may have had some serious problem in your life which kept you "awake" at night, searching for an answer when you should have been sleeping. Actually, you were probably on the verge of sleep but:

- You were completely relaxed
- You searched for solutions to your problem
- When you found a solution you reviewed its suitability thoroughly
- You might have "walked through," in your mind, the use of your idea
- If you met problems in using your idea, you mentally improved on it until it was ready to use without any of its former problems
- When you tried out your idea the next day it worked like a dream!

So you see, you may have been using Auto-Hypnosis for years without really knowing it! And if you have, you know how successful it can be.

Five Wealth-Builders Who Hit Big Money

To prove that Auto-Hypnosis really works, here are a number of actual results achieved by real-life Beginning Wealth-Builders, just like you and me. If they can do it, so can you!

CANNONS MAKE A BIG MONEY BOOM

Charlie T. was given a toy cannon for Fourth of July one year. He had so much fun with it that he decided to buy several more. But when he tried to find other cannons, he quickly learned that there weren't that many cannon makers around. In fact, at that time Charlie found that there were only four cannon makers in the entire United States!

Charlie decided that he *must* have the type of cannon he wanted. To get such a cannon, Charlie used the time just before going to sleep each night to explore the world of cannons. Using this easy form of Auto-Hypnosis, Charlie soon found that he could:

* Import the cannon from overseas
* Build the cannon himself
* Buy some parts; have other parts built

As he drifted off to sleep one night, Charlie T. decided that he would try to import more than one cannon of the type he liked. Once he had the cannons in hand he'd try to sell them by mail order. Using the book *Worldwide Riches Opportunities* as a guide, this is what Charlie did:

(1) Located overseas cannon makers
(2) Wrote each maker
(3) Worked out a suitable price
(4) Imported six cannons
(5) Sold all within a week
(6) Imported 1,000 more with the same result

Today Charlie T. is the fifth cannon builder in the U.S. and his business is booming. And how did Charlie T. prove out his business before investing a cent? By Auto-Hypnosis!

SELLING OLD ADS

Bill M. enjoys reading out-of-date back-issue magazines. Once, when he was extremely short of money, Bill decided to think over his cash problem while lying on the grass alongside a beautiful lake in northern Michigan. Since it was a warm, sunny summer day, Bill relaxed quickly after lying down on the grass.

As he lay there, trying to think of ways to obtain quick cash, the idea of trying to earn money from his reading hobby kept repeating itself to him. Suddenly he thought of the amusing ads which appeared in the magazines published in 1895, 1900, 1910, and so on. Perhaps the firms which ran those ads would be interested in having copies of them. Bill followed through on this idea and soon was:

* Collecting hundreds of old magazines
* Making a photo copy of old ads
* Sending the ad photo copy to the advertising manager of the company which ran the ad

- Charging $5 for one photo copy, and $50 for the page on which the ad originally appeared

Today Bill has a highly profitable mail-order business which he runs in his spare time and which nets him at least $100,000 a year. Why is such a simple idea—obtained under Auto-Hypnosis—so profitable? Because:

- All firms are interested in their old ads
- A price of $5, or even $50, is a small amount for any firm to pay
- Most firms will order hundreds of extra copies of ads, increasing the profit potential
- Companies pay their bills quickly
- There is hardly any overhead and very little labor expense in this business

So Auto-Hypnosis put Bill in Business. "And it keeps me successful," Bill says. "I still use my 'think-in-the-grass' sessions to give me new ideas for my business and personal life. You can't beat Auto-Hypnosis for generating, and proving out, good ideas!"

EUROPEAN REAL ESTATE PAYS OFF

If I could, I'd like to invite every one of my readers to travel throughout the world with me on my frequent business trips. But there are so many readers that they'd fill a whole fleet of planes. To make up for the trip we can't take together, let's *dry-run* a European trip right here.

You meet me at New York's JFK Airport about ninety minutes before takeoff. We check in, show our passports and health certificates, and receive details about the flight—gate number, our reserved-seat numbers (you pick the window seat; I like the aisle seat anyway), and loading time.

With these matters finished, we wander off to glance in shop windows and watch the tourists as they come and go. "Come on, friend," I say, "I'll buy you a bit of thirst quencher."

"Sure," you smile, "I'm thirsty and I could use a short one."

So we go upstairs to the modern cafe with its model airplanes, miniskirted waitresses, and chatter of happy talk.

We both order our favorite refreshment and start to talk.

"Ty," you say, "I've always wanted to get into real estate in Europe. I think there's money to be made in it."

"There sure is," I say, "Since we have a seven-hour trip ahead of us, why don't you try some Auto-Hypnosis on yourself instead of watching the movie?"

"That's exactly what I'll do," you say with a smile. "Drink up—it's nearly time."

Our plane is a big Boeing 747. We're sitting up front in the first-class section. You relax in the contoured seat while I explain a few details about the plane.

"How do you know these things?" you ask.

"Oh, I used to be a mechanical engineer," I say. "So I'm still interested in anything that's mechanical. And, an airplane such as this represents some of the most sophisticated engineering around. Why the very rug that you walk on is engineered—from a weight standpoint."

After a smooth takeoff you close your eyes and doze. I hope you're using Auto-Hypnosis. In an hour or so you awaken, just before the first refreshments are served.

"Let's go up to the lounge," I suggest. "We can have our drinks there."

"Sure," you reply.

We climb the circular staircase to the attractively decorated lounge. Taking seats, we order our drinks.

"While I was half asleep," you say after the first sip of your drink, "I could see the entire European land deal as clearly as though I were looking down from an airplane at 6,000 feet on a sparkling sunny day. The whole deal is very simple, Ty," you laugh.

"Let's hear what Auto-Hyposis told you," I grin, leaning back in the comfortable seat as our big Boeing 747, high above the Atlantic waves, races smoothly eastward toward Europe.

"This is what Auto-Hypnosis showed me I could do," you say.

(1) Start buying European land *now*

(2) Use a small, borrowed down payment to hold the land while the deal is progressing

(3) Since it takes a relatively long time (about a year) to buy European land, I can be advertising its sale while I'm buying

(4) Collect a bigger down payment for my "sale" than
I paid

(5) Use this down payment to pay off my down payment, hold the balance for down payments on
other land deals

(6) Continue working this deal wherever possible

I nod as you outline your plan. Its basic concept is
simple—but highly powerful, namely:

When you can corner the market on an item
whose price is rising rapidly, or for which there
is a growing demand, but a fixed or restricted
supply, time will turn your investment into profit.

As we're deplaning in London, I offer you some final
hints:

To make money in a real-estate deal such as the one
you developed during our flight, keep these facts in mind:

(1) Use as small a down payment as possible to control your purchase.

(2) Borrow the down payment—don't use your own
capital.

(3) Take immediate steps to sell out your interest in
the purchase.

(4) Be certain you have reliable legal advice and a
carefully written contract covering the deal.

(5) Sell as soon as you can, *at a profit.* Don't wait to
squeeze the last penny out of a deal—sell and go
on to the next deal which may be more profitable.

(6) Keep searching for new items on which you can
use this technique.

Typical items on which this approach works well include:

(A) Real estate
(B) Paintings
(C) Rare coins
(D) First editions of books
(E) Tapestries, rugs

Numerous readers of my books have made millions using
this approach to European and U.S. land and real-estate
deals. You can too!

TRAINING THE EDUCATED

Simon R. works on Wall Street but he's no longer in the stock market. Instead, he teaches well-educated men and women how to pass the various examinations to become registered representatives and other brokerage-house officials. While there are a number of schools teaching these subjects, Simon's school is extremely successful because of a technique he developed while under Auto-Hypnosis.

"I ride a local commuter bus," Simon explains, "and sometimes I go into this Auto-Hypnosis state while on the bus. Ideas become very clear to me and I direct my subconscious to put into action those ideas which seem worthwhile. It's amazing how powerful this system is. Once I direct my subconscious to 'run the idea' I find myself working like a demon to put the idea into action. I discovered the real power of this system a few years ago when I was trying to cure myself of inertia and procrastination. At that time I told my subconscious to '*Do it now*' while under Auto-Hypnosis. That very day I found myself propelled by an enormously positive drive to get everything done *now*. I've believed in the great power of Auto-Hypnosis ever since.

"So when I got the basic idea for the stockbrokers school I put Auto-Hypnosis to work on it to develop a new approach which would really sell to the well-educated people on Wall Street. Auto-Hypnosis immediately showed me that I needed:

(1) A fast, sure teaching method
(2) Courses given at the students' convenience

"The fast, sure teaching method was needed because the students are already well educated and they can't waste time learning useless theories. And I had to offer my courses at my students' convenience because they are active, busy people.

"Using Auto-Hypnosis during my bus rides between home and the office I developed my 'Instant Learning' method which puts ideas across rapidly and surely. Further, I decided to offer my courses in the evenings and on weekends."

Today Simon's school is so successful that he has a waiting list of thousands of students. Simon has gone public —i.e., sold stock in his school corporation to the public— and picked up more than a million dollars in working capital. Auto-Hypnosis put Simon in an unusual business which today is growing at an enormous rate.

A NO-CAPITAL WAY TO WEALTH SUCCESS

Morton P. called me one Sunday evening to ask for money and success advice.

"Ty," he said, "I'll summarize my problems as quickly as possible. I:

(1) Have *no* cash
(2) Am a poor credit risk
(3) Never ran a business
(4) Hate to work for others
(5) Often lose my temper
(6) Sometimes feel lazy
(7) Am over forty

"What," Morton wailed, "can I do to get rich fast?"
"Anything you want to do, Morton," I replied. "You just have to figure:

(1) What you want to do in life.
(2) When you want to reach your goal.
(3) Who can help you.
(4) How to achieve your wealth goal.

"The first three steps are the easiest, Morton. It's the fourth step that can give you problems. But let me give you a thought. That is:

"When you are low on cash and you want to start a business, seek a no-capital type of set up where you invest only your time, energy, and skill."

So if you're in a situation similar to Morton's, take these steps:

(1) Decide what you want to do
(2) Check to see if a no-cash deal is possible
(3) Investigate other arrangements

(4) Apply Auto-Hypnosis to yourself
(5) Go ahead with the deal

Now what kinds of businesses can be started with *no cash* you ask. Thousands, I reply. And here's the main characteristic of each such business:

> You can obtain the main commodity, i.e., the item you sell or service, of the business without making any investment until after you've sold the commodity.

The usual way businessmen refer to such an arrangement is by saying that you obtain the item you sell "on consignment." This means that the maker or supplier of the item is giving you 100 percent financing because *you don't put up a cent to get the item into your place of business.*

Now I'm sure you may be frowning a trifle as you read this because you have a number of key questions. Since I believe I know what most of these questions are, I'll present them below in concise question-and-answer form.

Q. Why would any product maker or manufacturer give me 100% financing?

A. Because he wants to sell his product or service.

Q. How long can I keep the item before selling it, without paying for it?

A. Forever, if necessary. Usually, though, you'll send it back if you don't sell it in one year.

Q. Must I lay out any cash to obtain the item I want to sell?

A. No, if you overlook the postage or phone bill on the order you place.

Q. My place of business, and some of the items in it, is damaged by fire. Who pays for the damaged items?

A. The maker of the items—*not you!*

Q. What businesses offer on-consignment arrangements for their products?

A. Here are a few you should study to see if the on-consignment arrangement applies in your area:

(1) Medical and technical books
(2) Paints and painting supplies

(3) Auto repair parts
(4) Certain real-estate properties
(5) Some mail-order items

Besides these there are hundreds of other items you can obtain without putting up a cent.

Q. Are there any other on-consignment type arrangements I might use?

A. Yes; some firms offer 180-, 210-, 270-, 300-, 330-, and 360-day on-consignment deals. While these are not quite the same as "forever," they do allow you to go into business quickly and with minimum investment.

Morton P. decided to sell medical books as the way to a quick fortune because he could get the books on consignment without putting up a dime. Then all he had to do was to find enough buyers to move a large enough number of copies to give him the income he sought. That's another secret of this method, namely:

> With a long allowable payoff time you should seek to sell as many units as possible to bring in a large sum of money with which you can work—such as by putting the money into other investments—until you have to pay for the items you sold.

Morton P. used Auto-Hypnosis again to find a way to sell medical books against the competition. He came up with two great ideas:

(1) Sell at a big discount
(2) Give his customers a longer time to pay

Using these Auto-Hypnosis developed ideas, Morton soon had zooming sales of medical books to local doctors, nurses, hospitals, medical schools, and libraries. Today Morton is the biggest medical-book dealer in his area and his income is over $200,000 a year. Yet he started without a cent and built his fortune using Auto-Hypnosis and hard work.

Never Neglect Auto-Hypnosis in Your Wealth Search

You have the money power of the ages right between your two ears. That magic power—Auto-Hypnosis—can turn your ambitions into big money today! So start now and get to work fast. Why wait when all you need do is go out and make a lot of that *big money* yours?

USEFUL BOOKS ON SELF-HYPNOSIS

Arons, H.—*Handbook of Self-Hypnosis,* Borden Publishing Co.

Arons, H.—*Speed Hypnosis,* Borden Publishing Co.

Caprio, F. and Berger J.—*Helping Yourself with Self-Hypnosis,* Parker Pub. Co.

Caprio, F.—*Programmed Course in Self-Hypnosis,* Prentice-Hall, Inc.

Douven, J.—*Powers of Hypnosis,* Stein & Day

Fielding, T.—*Auto-Suggestion You Can Use,* Borden Publishing Co.

Furst, A.—*Hypnosis for Salesmen,* Borden Publishing Co.

Le Cron, L.—*Self-Hypnotism: The Technique and Its Use in Daily Living,* Prentice-Hall, Inc.

Van Pelt, S.—*Secrets of Hypnotism,* Wehman Books.

seven

How to Use
OPM to Build
Your Fortune

In the last chapter I showed you how to get started in business without putting up a cent of your own. To do this I suggested that you "live on" the suppliers' capital, as Morton P. did. Since I want to make you as rich as possible as soon as possible, I'm now going to give you an entire chapter on how you can get rich using Other People's Money—OPM.

Borrowing Money Is Fun and Profitable!

If you have that old-fashioned idea that only broke or poor people borrow money, get rid of that idea right now because today money is borrowed by:

- The biggest and richest companies
- Millions of wealthy people
- Governments of many countries
- Millions of small businesses
- Nearly every man and woman who got rich recently

Borrowing money for business purposes is "in" like never before. Today people don't boast about how much money they have—instead they boast about how much they owe! No longer is it a shame or a disgrace to owe money. In this modern age, the more you owe to others for business deals, the bigger your position in the world!

"This can't be," you say. "Good people pay their debts and stay out of trouble."

"You're right—in a way," I reply. "But more **and** more people are borrowing larger and larger sums for business. So why don't you?"

Advantages of Borrowing OPM

When you *borrow money to make money*, you use one of the most powerful magic mind secrets known in the world today for building enormous wealth. All you need is a good idea to match to the money you borrow and you're off on a glorious road to great wealth—fast.

Other advantages of borrowing OPM include:

- You work harder and have a greater chance to hit it *big*
- With money in hand you can concentrate on the business aspects of each deal—improving your chances of success
- Money in the bank—even borrowed funds—gives you more confidence so you work relaxed and close more *big money* deals
- Cash on hand can help you work sharper deals—thus you may be able to obtain large discounts or more favorable prices
- Having money ready may allow you to buy a business, acquire materials, or otherwise capture a deal while your competition is fumbling around to find the needed cash
- Lastly, with cash in your hands, people chase *you*. This gives you independence, freedom of action, and the ability to make the best deals for yourself

Never overlook the importance of having money in your pocket—even OPM. It may seem silly but it's true that:

OPM can put you in a money-making state of mind— that is, you can earn more because you have more!

OPM is the magic that builds wealth in every country of the world—large, small, and in-between. Why should you remain poor when, with a little bit of OPM, you can become rich?

Know Your Sources of OPM

There are a large number of sources of OPM you can tap. These include:

- Banks of many types
- Finance companies
- Professional money lenders
- Insurance companies
- Financial brokers
- Venture-capital firms
- State industrial development authorities
- Small Business Administration
- The general public through a stock offering
- A restricted public through a "private offering"

Let's take a quick look at each of these methods to see how *you* can obtain OPM. As we progress with our study we'll see exactly how powerful OPM can be in *your* life.

Tap Your Bank for a Personal Loan

Your bank is your friend. Why? Because *your* bank:

- Wants your *loan* business
- Needs your *loan* business to earn profits
- Actively searches out *loans* to make
- Needs your *loan* business to survive
- Is willing to make deals with *you*
- Understands *you* and *your* problems
- Has plenty of *money* to lend

How do you approach *your* bank to borrow money? That's easy. All you do is:

(1) Visit your bank
(2) Ask for a personal loan application
(3) Take your application home
(4) Study the application
(5) Fill out your loan application
(6) Go back to the bank and sit down with a loan officer
(7) Tell him you are *not* asking for a loan but that
(8) You'd like to know *if* you applied for a loan with this application *if* it would be approved
(9) *Listen* attentively and make notes of what he tells you
(10) Obtain a new application and alter it to suit if he tells you he would *not approve* your loan
(11) Decide to apply for the loan if he tells you he *would approve* your loan application

"What about a business loan?" you ask. Try a personal loan first, I suggest, because:

- Personal loans are approved faster
- You are asked fewer questions
- There is a shorter credit check
- Many banks prefer personal loans
- Your loan officer will be friendlier
- You'll feel more welcome in the bank
- The whole deal is easier on you

So consider a personal loan *first*. Once you have such a loan, and know the ways of dealing with bank loan officers, you'll have less trouble obtaining a business loan at a later date.

How much can you obtain on a personal loan? Each state has its own regulations, but typical amounts you can borrow are up to $5,000 in some states and up to $7,500 in other states. These amounts should be enough to get you started in most small businesses.

Try a Business Loan from Your Bank

Once you get started in your business you can try a business loan from your bank. How much can you borrow on a business loan? There's no real limit when you deal with a large bank. For instance, you can borrow three, five, or ten million dollars from a large bank if your business is big enough to *repay* the loan.

But from a practical standpoint, the most a small business-man should look for is $5,000 to $30,000 for his first business loan. As time passes and your business improves, you should be able to increase this to $50,000 to $100,000 without trouble. The key to raising the amount the bank lends to you is given below.

Eight Sure-Fire Mind Secrets to Loan Success

You *can* borrow the money *you* need from a bank. Here are a number of sure-fire mind secrets to obtaining the money *you* need for your business:

(1) Open a checking account at the bank *before* you apply for a loan.

(2) Create a *good* image at the bank by becoming friendly with one or more loan officers.

(3) Try to refer other people to the bank, using a letter to do so, and being sure to send a carbon copy of your letter to the bank loan officer with whom you are the most friendly.

(4) Show activity in your checking account by writing a number of checks.

(5) Try to keep as large a balance as possible—even of bor-rowed money—in your checking account.

(6) *Never, never* allow one of your checks to "bounce"—i.e., be refused for payment because of low funds

(7) Forget your fear of banks—if you have any.

(8) Remember at all times that the average bank *wants* and *needs* your business.

Think positively about every bank! True, a bank may turn down your loan application today. But tomorrow the same bank may be pleading with you to borrow their money. Use the eight sure-fire mind secrets above and I guarantee you that you'll be able to borrow the OPM you need.

Put a Finance Company to Work for You

There are thousands of finance companies throughout the world. And many of these, as you probably know, are in the United States. Finance companies are:

- Usually readier to loan money than banks
- Often charge higher interest rates
- May not lend for as long a time
- Closer to business realities than some banks
- Sometimes limited in the amounts they can lend
- Becoming more respected

How can you obtain the names of a large number of finance companies and banks which may be ready to lend you money? Subscribe to the monthly newsletter, *International Wealth Success* for $24 per year. Also send for a copy of *Business Capital Sources,* priced at $15. Both the newsletter and book are available from IWS Inc., P.O. Box 186, Merrick, N. Y. 11566. With these big publications in hand you shouldn't have any trouble locating finance companies and banks that will lend you the money you need. The book also lists hundreds of other lenders and many mail-order loan sources. On page 233 of the book you are now reading, you will find "Helpful Money Books," a listing of several books to further help you.

"How much will a finance company lend me?" you ask. That depends on the kind of company you go to. Small, consumer-type finance companies lend up to a maximum of $7,500, depending on the state in which the company is located. But big, business-oriented finance companies will lend you up to $100 million, or more, if your business can support the repayments on the loan.

These big finance companies will lend you money for numerous different business uses, such as for:

- Operating capital
- Equipment purchase
- Building construction
- Factoring of accounts receivable
- Inventory loans

The best way to work with a large finance company is:

(1) Visit the finance company office
(2) Meet the key officials there
(3) Talk to them about what they can do for you
(4) Ask for a loan application
(5) Study the application
(6) Follow the same procedure as in Steps 6 through 11 given above for obtaining a bank loan

A finance company loan may be just the type you need to get the OPM that will put you in the millionaire class. Try a finance company today and see what happens!

Can a Professional Money Lender Help Me?

Professional money lenders are of several types. The ones you'll meet most often include:

- Money lenders acting for wealthy persons
- Individual wealthy people seeking to lend money
- Corporation representatives looking for good investments for corporate cash

The professional money lender is often a shrewd judge of potential profit situations. If he thinks your deal offers promise he may invest millions in it. But if he can't see much hope for your potential business he'll drop you and go running after something more promising. This is probably good for both of you because you won't be wasting any time on him.

Where can you find a list of professional money lenders? Refer to copies of *International Wealth Success* and *Business Capital Sources*, mentioned above.

Insurance Companies Are Loaded with OPM

The world's insurance companies have billions and billions of OPM which they want to invest. Much of this money is ready for you if you want to borrow for business or real estate investments. And, joy of joys, the interest rates and fees (if any) charged by insurance companies are often low. So you can get heaps and heaps of OPM with hardly any effort by placing your loan with an insurance company.

"How do I get a loan from an insurance company?" you ask. That's easy; just follow the same rules given above for banks. "But there's no insurance company near me," you say. Well, then:

> Write to the lender from who you wish to borrow, no matter what type of lender you have in mind—bank, finance company, insurance company, etc. You can carry on all your loan dealings by mail, if you wish.

For the names of insurance firms seeking to lend money, glance through copies of *International Wealth Success* and *Business Capital Sources*, mentioned above. Once you have these lists in front of you, it is easy to choose those firms with whom you'd like to deal.

See a Financial Broker for the Money You Need

Financial brokers—like real estate and marriage brokers—bring two people together for the closing of a deal they both desire. If you use a financial broker he will bring you, the borrower, together with a lender—such as a bank, a finance company, an insurance company, etc.

What are the advantages of using a financial broker? There are a number of advantages for you, including:

- Fewer problems dealing with lenders
- Less shopping around for your loan
- Quicker analysis of your chances for a loan
- Possibility of a lower interest rate

When you deal with a financial broker, he takes on the details of:

- Contacting one or more lenders
- Presenting your case to the lender
- Arguing, if necessary, over interest rates
- Filling out the necessary papers
- Settling any minor problems which arise

"Does this service cost *me* anything?" you ask. It certainly does. You can't expect a financial broker to spend, free of charge, his time and energy on getting you a loan. But the fee you pay a financial broker will be nominal—certainly not more than $50 per $1,000 borrowed—i.e., 5 percent, and often less.

"Will the financial broker get anything from the lender?" Yes, he will. "How much?" That depends on the lender, the size of your loan, the reputation of the financial broker, etc. Generally the commission the financial broker earns from the lender is a little less than the commission he charges you.

How to "Beat the System"—Honestly

"Ty," you say, "I don't want to pay these guys a commission. Is there any way I can get around this?" Yes, there is.

You can become a financial broker yourself! "And how much will that cost me?" you ask. Just $99.50. All you need do is take the *Financial Broker-Finder-Business Broker-Business Consultant Program* available from IWS Inc., P.O. Box 186, Merrick, N.Y. 11566 for $99.50. This program will give you the basic facts you need to get started in these interesting, challenging, and profitable professions, the most important of which is the financial broker profession.

Why do I recommend that you consider becoming a financial broker? Because:

- You'll quickly learn who's lending money
- Profits can be earned by you rapidly
- Hundreds of OPM sources will be available to you
- Your money know-how will zoom
- Borrowing OPM will become routine to you
- New business ideas will flow into your office
- People will have greater respect for you
- Plenty of people (both lenders and borrowers) will seek you out to do business with you

You can't lose when you become a financial broker. Also, you can act as a

- Finder
- Business Broker
- Business Consultant

The above program gives you the forms, outlines, loan applications, and complete instructions for getting started today. Try it now and see.

Venture-Capital Firms Have Bundles of OPM

A *venture-capital firm* is a company set up to lend money to small, struggling firms which need OPM backing for a good idea. Today there are probably several hundred venture-capital firms in the United States, and a like number in Europe. Japan has some two hundred.

When you check into venture-capital firms you quickly learn that they lend money in several ways, including:

- An outright loan
- Purchase of your company stock
- Buying of your company bonds
- Financing machinery and equipment
- Payment of current expenses

What does a venture-capital firm look for when checking out new loans for struggling small firms? Typically the venture-capital firm looks for:

- Future profitability
- Ambitious management
- Salable idea or product
- Large market for the idea or product
- An aggressive marketing force

There are hundreds of experienced and capable venture-capital firms—many of which are listed in *International Wealth Success* and *Business Capital Sources*—actively seeking to lend you OPM. So if you have a good idea that you want to promote actively, get in touch with a venture-capital firm.

Try a State Business Loan

All of the states have an industrial development board of some type which encourages business activities in the state. Such a development board can:

- Arrange 100% financing of plants
- Lend money for equipment and machinery
- Finance worker training
- Suspend taxes for a number of years

To obtain a list of the state industrial development boards in each state, and the territories of the United States, send $5 to IWS, Inc., P.O. Box 186, Merrick, N.Y. 11566. This list gives the name, address, and telephone number (for most boards). You should find it helpful if you want to borrow OPM from your state.

Important Notice. Some state business loan agencies lend *only* to established businesses or *only* to out-of-state businesses they are trying to attract. So don't be discouraged if you're told that loans are unavailable to new or yet-to-be established businesses. Just try another loan source—such as a bank, financing company, private lender, etc.

Is the SBA Your Source of OPM?

The Small Business Administration run by the United States Government is an excellent source of low-interest business loans— *if you have been rejected for a loan by your local bank.* This means that SBA won't lend you money if a bank will.

Where can you obtain information about SBA loans? Refer to *Business Capital Sources,* mentioned above, for a full description of each type of SBA loan available to you. These loans include:

- Disaster loans
- Inventory loans
- Real-estate loans
- Equipment loans
- Refinance loans
- And many other types of loans

The SBA loan you apply for today can put you on easy street within just a few years. And, as this is being written, the SBA is liberalizing its loan policies so that more people can borrow larger sums of money. The new rules will probably:

- Require fewer credit references

- Extend repayment periods
- Reduce the interest rate
- Help people borrow more

Get the information you need on SBA loans now. Then go out and borrow the money you need. You'll never be sorry you did.

Sell Your Company Stock to the Public

Every source of OPM we've mentioned up to now involves *paying back* the money you borrow. On most loans you must repay every month, though on some loans you can repay once a year. But the important point is this:

Business loans must be repaid. The repayments you make can seriously reduce your spendable income until you pay off the amount you owe, plus the interest on the borrowed money.

When you sell stock to the public you are in a much better position because:

- You can obtain large amounts of OPM
- There is *no* need to repay the money
- No credit check is made
- You can use the money for any business purpose
- Dividends can be paid whenever you choose

"Can I really sell the stock in my company to the public?" you ask. Certainly you can, if you're organized as a corporation. Thousands of companies sell their stocks to the public every year. "How much can I get for my company from a stock offering?" Any amount you need from $50,000 to $50 million, or more.

But for your first stock offering I recommend that you limit yourself to a Regulation A Offering—i.e., that you sell only enough stock to give a cash flow to the company of $500,000, or less. Using a Regulation A Offering will limit the paperwork and the legal details involved in your stock offering. Also, you'll "get your feet wet" in the easiest way possible, without a large number of legal problems.

Personally, I think that selling stock to the public is one of the best ways possible for you to latch onto a large amount of OPM in a hurry. Check out *your* chances in the IWS Financial Broker Program mentioned above. This program contains much useful information (forms, rules, procedures, etc.) for taking a company public. So learn today how you can obtain up to millions of dollars of OPM to put to work to make your ideas earn money for yourself and your stockholders!

Private Stock Offerings Can Help Too

A *private placement* of stock occurs when you sell most of your stock to one, or a few (usually less than 25) buyers. Thus, there are *investment bankers* (really high-class lenders) who might buy some of the stock in your company, if they think you have a profitable business in the making. Or you might sell $10,000 worth of stock to each of 20 investors, giving you a total of $200,000 in cash.

Usually, a private placement is more difficult to make than a public offering. Why? Because the people in charge of the private funds will inspect every part of your company—from basement to boardroom—over and over. You (usually) really have to "sweat" for your money. Then, once you get the OPM you need this way, your business operations are carefully checked on. In fact, you'll usually have a representative of the investment banker on the board of directors of your company.

By comparison, the wider ownership of a public stock issue, reduces (for most firms) the problems of close supervision of your company which accompany the usual private offering. That's why I recommend that you consider the public issue way to large sums of OPM.

OPM Is Your Fast Way to Wealth

This book gives you hundreds of magic mind secrets for building your fortune. Of all these secrets, OPM is probably the:

* Most widely used
* Broadest in scope

- Easiest to apply
- Best for you and me

But as with any other powerful technique, you must apply it wisely. Careless use of OPM could put you into debt when you should be earning a profit. So don't borrow OPM unless:

- Your business deal is a proven one
- You know how to handle money
- You have two or more ways of earning money to re-pay what you borrowed
- Your confidence in yourself is high

In our next chapter we tell you about money Beginning Wealth-Builders (BWBs) just like yourself who used OPM to build enormous fortunes. Why not move on to the next chapter now to see how others have made wealth and happiness theirs, using the magic power of borrowed money.

eight

How to
Find Riches
Wherever You Go

Sometimes people turn away from money, saying "I want the non-material riches of this world." Great, I say. I love these riches too. Riches like:

- Birds twittering on a spring morning
- A calm lake on a summer evening
- The beauty of a fall sunset
- White clouds skimming through the sky
- The soft crunch of forest soil underfoot
- The smell of pine trees and pine needles
- A desert and its ear-shattering silence

You could probably name two or three dozen more riches like these which particularly appeal to you. That's wonderful because it shows that you are an intelligent, sensitive person. Yet during my business travels all over the world, one key fact which I have observed everywhere, amongst all peoples, is this:

Having money helps you enjoy more of the non-material aspects and parts of your life!

So, good friend, there's little chance to escape the fact that:

- Having money helps you live better
- Having money gives you the chance to enjoy more things in life
- Having money is good for you, for me, for all sensible people

Find Money Wherever You Go!

There's a strange power called *serendipity* in the lives of many wealth-builders. Serendipity is the ability to make *fortunate and unexpected* discoveries by accident, and to find valuable and useful things while you are not consciously seeking them. The magic power of serendipity is the result of:

- Taking *action* in life
- *Seeking* the good things in business
- *Working* hard

AND

- *Being* in the *right* place at the right *time*

You can put serendipity into your fortune building activities by applying the steps given in this chapter. Putting serendipity to work for yourself can:

- Bring OPM into your business
- Attract new customers to you
- Help you find a top executive job, if that's what you want
- Pull good luck into your life and chase out bad luck

Let's see how you can get this magic power of serendipity going for yourself right now!

Get Ready for Instant Riches

Serendipity won't come into your life unless you invite it in. And how do you go about the inviting? That's easy. You:

- Decide, in general terms, what you want, or need in life
- Choose the best way, or ways to get what you want
- Act to achieve your objectives

Thus, to get serendipity to work for you:

You must put yourself in a position, state of mind, and physical readiness such that you are ready when serendipity beckons!

What this rule means is that you must *work* at being ready for serendipity whenever she calls. Why? Because if you aren't ready when serendipity calls:

- You won't recognize or hear the call
- You won't be ready to get the most from what is offered you
- Your bad luck may increase, while your good luck decreases

So while serendipity can bring you riches beyond belief in a matter of moments, *you must be ready to receive these riches!* In this chapter I will show you exactly how to get ready.

Decide What You Want

Let's say you have a slight problem deciding what you want in life. How can you overcome this problem? That's easy—use the eight-step magic form below, filling in the blanks that apply to you. Use this form *now*, if you want outstanding results.

MY WHAT-I-WANT FORM

Money

1. By ＿＿＿＿＿＿＿＿ I want to have $＿＿＿＿ in
   　　　　(date)　　　　　　　　　　(amount)
   business capital.
2. I will obtain the $＿＿＿＿ by ＿＿＿＿＿＿＿＿
   　　　　　　(amount)　　　(state how you'll get

   ＿＿＿＿＿＿.
   the money)

3. By _____ I want to have $_____ in
          (date)   (amount)
   personal savings.
4. By _____ I want to have $_____ in
          (date)   (amount)
   personal investments.

Business or Job

1. By _____ I want to own, and run, a
          (date)
_____ business.
   (state name)
2. By _____ I want to be a _____
          (date)   (name job
_____ of a company.
   title)
3. By _____ I want to be earning $_____
          (date)   (amount)
   per year in a business or top executive job.
4. By _____ I want to own, or be able to
          (date)
   lease without straining my finances, the following for
   my personal pleasure and use: _____,
                                  (name of item)

_____, _____,
  (name of item)   (name of item)

_____, _____.
  (name of item)   (name of item)

Study this form carefully after you've finished it. Why? Because it will set your mind so you are mentally ready for serendipity when it comes into your life. For, as the man said: "Luck comes to those who prepare for it."

Three Who Decided What They Wanted

To show *you* how you can get the magic power of serendipity to work for you, I'd like to tell you about three Beginning Wealth-Builders (BWBs) who did just that for themselves. Please read their stories carefully because they may contain some useful ideas for you.

OPM FROM APPLES

Bernie L. wanted to grow apples—nice big, luscious, succulent apples that he could sell throughout the world. But, like many other BWBs, Bernie:

- Had a profitable idea
- Knew how to make his idea work
- Was ready to work hard
- *Didn't have a dime to invest*

What to do? Bernie's answers to this question were:

(1) Borrow from a bank
(2) Borrow from a finance company
(3) Sell stock to the public

Bernie tried the first two without luck. Visiting banks and finance companies only wasted time, he soon found, because:

- His business wasn't established yet
- His credit rating was poor
- Banks didn't like apples as a business venture

So Bernie decided to try to sell stock to the public. To do this, he:

- Prepared a prospectus or description of the apple business he wanted to start
- Had a dozen copies of the prospectus run off
- Contacted several stockbrokers
- Presented his story to each broker

Bernie seemed to be drawing blanks until he talked to the sixth broker on his list. As Bernie told his story he could see the broker's eyes widening with interest. Also, the broker was nodding in agreement, instead of trying to shush him and gently eject him from the office as the other brokers had.

"I can't sell your stock, Bernie," the broker said with a smile. "But I can set you up in the apple orchard business."

"How?" Bernie asked, excited at the prospect of finally getting started.

"My family left me a twenty-four-hundred acre apple

orchard and I've been trying for years to get someone to run
it for me. I think you're just the man I need."

"If I am, you'll have to make the deal worthwhile,"
Bernie said.

"That I will," the broker replied.

Now here's the deal they worked out. Bernie:

- Was given 800 acres of land in place of pay for
  his first three years' work
- Is to operate the 2,400-acre orchard
- Will receive 25% of the profits of the complete
  orchard for the first three years
- Will receive 50% of profits thereafter
- Was given a $100,000 loan for operating capi-
  tal on signing the contract

Today Bernie owns the entire orchard and is worth
more than $1 million. Why? Because he was ready when
serendipity called. True, Bernie wasn't able to borrow the
money he needed, nor sell the stock to get the capital he
sought. But:

Being ready to work a deal enables you to move
swiftly when a variation of the deal (serendipity) develops.

So pattern yourself after Bernie. That is:

- Get ready *in advance*
- *Work* towards your goal
- Use your *ingenuity*
- *Keep pushing*—day and night

OPM FROM A SIMPLE LIST

Charlie K. had a clear-cut ambition in life. All he
wanted to do was to own a collection of white doves, prize
pigeons, and similar beautiful birds which he could enjoy
and rent out for weddings, banquets, dinners, and other
functions. But Charlie had a problem which some of my
readers may also have—*he didn't have any money to invest
in his potential business.*

What could he do? I'm about to give you one of
several powerful money techniques which can be used by

Beginning Wealth-Builders (BWBs). Here's what Charlie K. did. He:

(1) Checked his chances of obtaining a loan at several banks

(2) Did the same at a number of finance companies

(3) Made complete notes of exactly what he needed to have his loan application approved

(4) Took action to obtain approval of the loan application

Now what did Charlies K. need to have his loan approved? He needed:

(a) A properly filled out loan application

(b) Complete details of his credit history

(c) Information on his address, phone number, employer, etc.

(d) At least one—and preferably two—acceptable cosigners

The cosigners required by the banks and finance companies Charlie K. visited had to:

(1) Be willing to pay off the loan if Charlie couldn't

(2) Have enough income to make the monthly loan repayments in the event Charlie K. couldn't

But Charlie K. didn't have any friends who could, or would, cosign his loan application for him. So he had to turn to someone else for help. This he did by writing to IWS Inc., P.O. Box 186, Merrick, N.Y. and subscribing to *International Wealth Success.* This monthly newsletter often lists professional loan cosigners who, for a modest fee, will cosign a suitable loan application. Charlie soon had his professional cosigners, plus much other useful information and lots of considerate help from the IWS staff. Today his bird business is booming and Charlie is delighted with the results. Why? Because Charlie K. was ready when serendipity called in the form of a published list of loan companies.

SELLING WHAT YOU DON'T OWN

It may seem silly, but more people get rich selling what they "don't own" than those who sell what they *do* own. "How does that work?" you ask.

The answer is easy. Further, the answer gives you the second of numerous powerful financing and borrowing techniques presented throughout this book. But I warn you now:

> The selling what you "don't own" technique is not for the timid, the unsure, or the frightened people of this world—instead it is for the brave, the adventurous, and the strong.

"Just what is this sell-what-you-'don't own' technique?" you ask. Here it is. You:

(1) Borrow money to buy a going business of some kind
(2) Sell part, or all, of the business to someone else
(3) Pay off your debt
(4) Keep the profit for yourself
(5) Continue operating the business if you didn't sell all of it

Now let's see how this system works in actual business practice. We'll use *you* as the example, if you don't mind!

Let's say you'd like to own a small, intimate island-style hotel and hideaway in the Caribbean. But you don't have the money for a down-payment. Yet you're so enthused about the idea that you regularly watch the ads and real-estate agency offerings. One day—*zap!* Serendipity steps in and you spot an ad for a place that is everything you ever dreamed you wanted.

Quickly you scrape together a few dollars and jet off to "your" hideaway. Once there you know this is the place for you because it has a:

• Main hotel building
• Twenty guest cottages
• Restaurant and cafe
• Boat marina

Not only do you like the place, your analysis of its business potential is highly promising. You see a net income of $100,000 per year as a definite possibility within a year or two. But, as always, there's a problem. You need at least $50,000 cash to take the place over. And you don't have that kind of money. What to do? Here's one approach:

(1) Study the profit potential of the business
(2) Prepare income and expense plans for the business as you see its future, for each year for the next five years
(3) Determine how you can sell off part of the property after you take it over
(4) Compute the income from the sell off
(5) List the expected pay off dates for any loans you'd have to obtain to take over the property or business
(6) With your financial plans neatly prepared, visit local banks, finance companies, and other lenders; discuss the possibility of obtaining a loan
(7) Accept a loan if it is offered to you

Using this approach you obtain a $50,000 loan from an insurance company to take over your hideaway. Once you have possession you:

• Sell the guest cottages for $100,000
• Lease the restaurant and cafe
• Lease the boat marina

Advances on the two leases amount to $10,000, giving you a total cash income of $110,000. You pay off the $50,000 loan and keep the $60,000 balance for operating capital. Thus, you've sold what you "don't own" and come out way ahead, all on OPM, and serendipity.

Attract Good Luck to Yourself

Serendipity works for those who work for their goals in life. I can't emphasize this point too strongly. Why does good luck, i.e., serendipity, come to those who work hard for their goals? Because those who prepare to achieve their goals:

• Are favored by the odds
• Seek the successful situations
• Find money while others just dream
• Have money offered to them
• Are busier and happier
• Contribute more to the world

Dreaming is the start of any wealth-building program, but action is the actual work of your program. We all need dreams to inspire us but none of us can build wealth without positive, directed action.

Mary T. spent years studying and preparing herself for a successful career as the owner of a chain of women's clothing stores. During her preparation Mary worked in numerous stores, learning the important facts about the business. Thus, when a highly profitable store came on the market for sale, Mary was quickly able to judge its potential. But, as with so many other BWBs, Mary didn't have enough cash to buy the store.

What to do? Mary went the usual route, trying banks, finance companies, and other lenders. But she had no luck.

Then she heard of the compensating-balance type of loan. With this type of loan Mary could pyramid loans at large city banks. Here's how:

(1) Borrow the maximum amount allowed by your state on a signature loan—usually $5,000 or $7,500.

(2) Use the amount received as a compensating-balance in a business checking account in your bank.

(3) Borrow from your bank using the compensating-balance as collateral—in the usual commercial bank you can borrow up to five times your compensating-balance.

(4) Use the funds from your compensating-balance loan to buy the business you seek, or

(5) Deposit the funds from your first compensating-balance loan into a second bank and negotiate a second compensating-balance loan at the second bank.

Let's look at this method more closely. At the same time we'll see what Mary did.

Pyramid Serendipity to Riches

Mary T. borrowed $7,500 on a signature loan because this is the easiest type of loan for an employed person to obtain. Also, $7,500 is the largest amount a person may borrow on a personal signature loan in her state.

Using the $7,500 as a compensating balance, Mary borrowed

five times that amount, or $37,500 from her commercial bank. Taking $35,000 of this money, she opened another compensating-balance account in another commercial bank and borrowed five times her balance or $175,000.

With the $175,000 she purchased the women's clothing store. Since she knew the business, Mary soon had a steady income which was enough to support her while she paid off the debts she had incurred. Today Mary owns an entire chain of profitable, growing stores. Thus, the magic power of serendipity combined with the compensating-balance technique built a quick fortune for an attractive young woman.

Catch the Good Things in Life

Serendipity is a marvelous power for you to pursue. Why? Because when you pursue this power you *can* catch it. And when you do catch serendipity, you'll latch onto many of the good things in life. And why shouldn't you have the best of everything? You deserve the best, you know!

As the author of this and four other money books, which are listed at the beginning of this book, I am your *good* friend. As such, I want to see you succeed quickly and spectacularly.

Why can I say I want to see you "make it big"? Because, as the man said, "I've made it myself." Having made my bundle several times over, I harbor no petty envy, jealousy, or other silly feelings about others who are making theirs. Today I get my kicks from seeing my clients make their bundle quickly, easily, and happily. So please read the books I recommend and take your first steps toward *great* wealth!

When you seek advice from good publications you set a positive force in motion in your life. This force, when combined with serendipity, can help you catch *all* the good things in life. Why lead a second-rate existence when, with a little effort, you can live like a king? Follow the advice in this book and you'll soon have everything you want in life. Why? Because:

Nothing is impossible when you choose your goals, prepare to succeed, and then work to achieve your objectives.

Thus, your key to the best in life can be summarized in just a few words:

Choose (your goals)
Prepare (to succeed)
Work (to achieve)

Turn Your Dreams Into Money

Money *isn't* everything, but money is important in all our lives. Almost anyone can scrape along on a small amount of money. But who wants to just scrape along?

There's a lot more to life than just existing. Most of the good things in your life, and in mine:

* Depend upon our dreams for realization
* Are achievable with some hard work
* Make everyone happier
* Require money for their use

When you turn your dreams into money you begin to take hold of the good things in life. And one key factor in turning *your* dreams into money is serendipity.

Serendipity is more powerful than any of us realize—until we see it at work. Clem L. learned this when he turned his dreams into money.

Clem wanted to sell tests which would help people check their knowledge by mail. "Who'd ever buy a mail-order test?" you ask. Thousands of executives, businessmen, and similar people here and abroad do.

Clem's dream was to sell 500,000 tests per year at $1 each. This would turn his dream into $500,000 per year. "Could it be done?" you ask. Certainly! In fact, with a little help from serendipity, Clem was able to double his dream in three years. Here's how.

Build Your Income Fast

Clem's dream was to sell tests that any executive or business-man could use to:

- Check his business know-how
- Help update his business information
- Use as a guide to courses he should take in a college or business school
- Otherwise update his general knowledge

Clem believed he could sell these tests both to companies and individuals. The advantages of selling to companies, as Clem saw them, were:

- Companies buy in large lots
- A firm pays fast
- There are few bad debts
- Repeat business is always possible
- The business is easily expanded
- International sales are possible

But there were also advantages in selling to individuals, namely:

- People would tell others about the tests
- Some people would show the tests to their firm, possibly increasing sales
- The tests would help many people

Take Action Today for Results Tomorrow

Clem took action immediately because:

- He *believed* in his idea
- By acting he was moving *forward*
- It would be *easy* to correct errors
- He would soon *know* if his idea was salable

To get moving on the proving of his idea, Clem:

- Prepared one sample page of a typical test
- Obtained a list of company names and addresses free from his local library
- Wrote a simple letter describing his test, and the prices he was charging

- Addressed envelopes to the company training director, using the library list
- Had his letter and sample test printed
- Mailed the letter and sample to 100 firms

The response to Clem's mailing was enormous. Thirty-one companies ordered tests, forcing Clem to finish writing his first test for which he had only one sample page. (That's a return of 31/100, or 31 percent. Most mail-order operators can get rich on a 3 percent return.)

Then serendipity stepped in. Several of the companies which *didn't* order tests on the first mailing wrote to:

- Ask Clem to edit similar tests which they had been using
- Prepare *special* tests for them
- Print their tests
- Correct their tests

So, in a matter of just days, Clem's idea expanded from a single business of selling tests by mail order to several other profitable, related businesses—all because serendipity stepped in *when Clem was ready!* Today Clem has a booming business here and abroad selling all sorts of testing services to firms and individuals. At this writing his sales are more than $1 million a year and they're still growing. That's not bad in three years!

Serendipity *can* be *your* answer to greater wealth, *sooner.* Put the hints in this chapter to work today and watch your wealth grow and grow!

And while you're considering serendipity, don't overlook the master money keys to using OPM to build wealth which are given to you in this chapter. These powerful techniques work with—and without—serendipity. So while you may reject serendipity (and I think you're making a *big* mistake if you do) you can still use the practical loan methods I give you!

nine

Putting More
Zest Into Your
Wealth-Building Skills

Several times earlier in this book I told you that my strongest and longest-lasting ambition in life is *to make you— my reader—rich.* And, friend, I'd like to say right now:

Hundreds and hundreds of readers of my money books have written me saying: "Your methods really work. I'm rich today because I read several of your books and put your methods to work for myself!"

Since I'm so interested in making *you* rich I'm putting every mind magic technique I know into this book. And I'm convinced that one of these will be right for you!

Tap an Infinite Source of Zest

Zest is an abundance of energy in yourself which makes you:

- Do it *now*
- Create new wealth ideas

- Take action on your ideas
- Keep pushing toward success

You can tap an infinite source of zest for business and your personal life if you follow the hints in this chapter. And, along the way, you might make yourself a millionaire!

Your infinite source of zest gains its energy (which it then transmits to you) from:

- Your knowledge of people
- Your ability to predict people's actions
- Your grasp of the future

When you can use your knowledge to learn how people will act, you lead a challenging and exhilarating life. Now here's how to learn what people might do.

Analyze People Quickly and Easily

One of the fastest and surest ways for you to analyze people is by studying their handwriting. You've no doubt heard of handwriting analysis. What most people haven't heard is that handwriting analysis is:

- Used by large firms to check personnel
- Extremely accurate and fast
- Costs nothing but some time
- Can be learned in a few weeks
- Usable in every business situation

From Rags to Riches in a Year

Sid R., was a gardener in a hospital two years ago. Today he sits behind his shiny new desk in his own factory. Two years ago Sid earned $400 per month; today he's earning $10,000 per month, not counting his almost-unlimited expense account covering first-class travel, hotels, meals, entertainment, and so on. And how did Sid move so fast in such a short time? He used handwriting analysis. Here's how.

Sid always wanted a business of his own, yet his low salary as a hospital gardener prevented him from building up enough savings to get started. So Sid went around depressed and discouraged. What Sid needed was a source of zest which would perk him up and get him to take action.

One day Sid saw a book on handwriting analysis in the hospital library. Borrowing the book, Sid began to read it. He was entranced and, within a few days, he analyzed his own handwriting. This analysis showed Sid that he was:

* Capable, alert, intelligent
* Ambitious, hard-working
* Blocked from success in his present job
* Able to make big money

Sid was both elated and depressed with his findings. To check the accuracy of his findings, Sid ran handwriting analyses on several friends. He was amazed at the accuracy of the results.

While gardening the next day, Sid had a wonderful idea. Why not turn his handwriting analysis to a profitable business use? Being able to analyze people quickly and easily through their handwriting could certainly be a business asset.

Learn the Truth About Business Deals

Sid decided that his first need was capital. And since he didn't have any savings, this meant that Sid's capital would have to come from other people, i.e., it would have to be borrowed.

So Sid filled out an application for a bank loan. He took it to the bank and discussed his money needs ($5,000 cash) with the loan officer. As Sid expected, his loan application was turned down. To gain a further insight into the real reasons for the turndown of his loan application, Sid asked the loan manager to *write out* his findings. The loan manager consented and did just that.

Analyzing the loan officer's handwriting in the turndown, Sid found that the loan officer was:

* Basically insecure
* Disliked ambitious people
* Unhappy in his job

So the truth about this business deal was that Sid was turned down more because of the *personality* of the person he was dealing with than because of the actual facts involved. This brings us to an important business concept, namely:

> People will often stand in your way because they don't want to see you succeed—to block you they'll cite so-called "facts."

Knowing this characteristic of people, you can try to get around it, just as Sid did. How? By using your head.

Combine Your Zest and Brain Power

Studying his analysis of the loan officer, Sid decided that the situation might be improved if he could:

• Make the loan officer feel more secure
• Play down his own ambitions
• Try to make the loan officer feel happier

So Sid went back to the *same* loan officer and used his zest for the loan and his brain power to convince the loan officer to approve the loan.

Sid achieved his goal of having the loan approved by:

(1) Telling the loan officer that banks offered the greatest job security in the world, as shown by various employment records.

(2) Saying little about what he, Sid, wanted to do in life and listening to the loan officer's dreams (he, incidentally, also wanted to own his own business).

(3) Taking the loan officer out to lunch and telling him how lucky he was (a) not to be in a hospital, jail, or sanitarium, (b) how lucky he was to be working for a big, well-respected bank which offered him a secure but exciting future.

Within an hour after making his second application, Sid's loan was approved. With his $5,000 check in hand, Sid started a lawn-care (mowing, fertilizing, gardening, etc.) business in his spare time.

Using his knowledge of handwriting analysis and the zest it provided him, Sid soon expanded his business to include:

- Swimming-pool construction and maintenance
- Window and building cleaning
- Factory grounds and building maintenance
- Home expansion and repair

In each business Sid was able to work a better deal because his knowledge of handwriting analysis enabled him to "read" the character of each person with whom he was doing business. Today Sid's take-home pay from his businesses is more than $120,000 a year!

You can combine *your* zest and brain power just the way Sid did and make *big money*. Try it now and see!

Use Other Character Analysis Techniques

To learn how other character analysis techniques are used, come with me, friend, for a year's round of business trips. We'll jet first class together from New York east to London, Paris, Rome, Berlin, Hamburg, Cairo, Athens, and perhaps, Moscow during the months of January and March. February we'll reserve for southern trips to Miami, San Juan, Saint Thomas, Aruba, Venezuela, Colombia, Brazil, Argentina, and Peru. You'll return bronzed and relaxed.

During April, May and June we'll travel west to Chicago, San Francisco, Los Angeles, San Diego; north to Toronto and Montreal; southwest to Atlanta, Dallas, Houston, San Antonio, El Paso, Phoenix, Tucson; further west to Honolulu, Guam, Midway, Manila, Tokyo, Hong Kong.

In each city you'll stay at the best hotels and eat in the finest restaurants. And I'll introduce you to my business friends and associates. You'll quickly see that these successful business people—like yourself—are:

- Ambitious
- Alert
- Active
- Thinkers
- Planners
- Analyzers
- Highly motivated
- Quick-witted
- Fast workers
- Adroit talkers

You'd also learn another important fact, namely:

Successful business people the world over use hundreds of different character-analysis techniques. These techniques vary from hunch to advanced psychoanalysis.

"Hunch works best for me," you say. But hunches can be misleading, can get you into trouble. What most folks need is a more scientific approach, such as:

- Handwriting analysis
- Supervised character analysis
- Executive personality definition
- Speed color tests of personality traits
- Lie-detector examination of personality
- Face-to-face psychiatry
- On-the-couch psychoanalysis

On these seven techniques the fastest, simplest, cheapest, and most widely used technique, you'll quickly find, is handwriting analysis. As we travel together you'll find wealthy business people everywhere using handwriting analysis to:

- Assess job applicants
- Analyze business associates
- Size up competitors
- Learn the real truth about business deals
- Gather other useful business information

You'd soon grow, I think, to have complete faith in handwriting analysis for business purposes. And, I believe, you'd want to learn how to use handwriting analysis in your own business deals, particularly after seeing how the wealthy people of this world work and play.

Start *Now* to Use Handwriting Analysis

To begin using handwriting analysis you must know something about its methods and procedures. Now I'm not going to try to teach you all you need to know—we don't have the needed space in this book. Instead, I've listed at the end of this chapter sixteen good books on handwriting analysis. Borrow one or more of these from your local library, or buy those you'd like to have on hand for reference. I recommend that you keep at least *three different* reference books on handwriting analysis on hand at all times. With this number of references on hand you should be able to solve any of the routine problems you meet.

Now start studying. To improve your skills in handwriting analysis, analyze:

* Your own handwriting (you'll learn something!)
* Friends' and relatives' handwriting
* Business associates' handwriting

Keep at your studies until you feel competent enough to make fast, accurate handwriting analyses. Then you'll be ready to use this technique to earn *big money!*

Apply Body Language Signals

Body language is the technique of "reading" another's mind by analyzing his bodily motions and positions. Most of us "read" some *body language* signals without realizing we are applying this valuable and profitable technique. Thus, when a man cups his hand over his mouth while talking, we sense that he's trying to keep his words secret from everyone except us.

There are many other, more subtle, body language signals than cupping a hand over the mouth which we may, or may not, read. Much depends on our sensitivity (or lack of it) to other people and their problems.

When combined with handwriting analysis, body language can give you a valuable insight into the minds and actions of other people.

To help you learn more about body language and its use, I've listed a few books on this subject at the end of this chapter. Study these books and apply what you learn in the same way I described for handwriting analysis. Master both these techniques and you'll be amazed at the power over other people which you'll develop. Few business problems will ever stop you!

Three Who Made It Big

If you've read any of my earlier money books, you know that:

- Every technique given has been used successfully by myself before being recommended to you
- A technique must earn *at least* five times its cost before I'll recommend it to you
- Only *completely honest* techniques are ever recommended to you
- Practical procedures—no high-blown theories—are the only methods I use and recommend to you
- You *must* be able to get rich fast from my techniques or I won't bother to tell you about them

Now I'm ready to tell you about three people, just like yourself, who used my practical, profitable, and proven mind magic techniques. You'll learn from them exactly how you, too, can make big money fast.

Mail-Order Way to Wealth

Susan T. wanted to work at home because she was a widow with four small children. Exploring various businesses, she soon found that the only one which would allow her to stay home was mail order.

Since Susan didn't know anything about mail order, she looked around for a college or school at which she could learn mail order. No schools in her area offered a course. However, she heard of the IWS Ten-Step Mail-Order Way to Wealth and sent for information. She quickly learned that this $99.50 program:

- Was a self-study guide to mail order
- Gave remarkably complete hints
- Was easy to use and put into action
- Awarded an attractive certificate of completion
- Could make money for her

Sending her $99.50 to IWS Inc. at Box 186, Merrick, N.Y. 11566, Susan T. soon had her program. She finished it in a few weeks and went to work on starting her business.

Pick Your Money Path and Run!

Using her program as a guide, Susan picked American flags for home and autos as her product. The reasons why Susan didn't pick just one type of flag to sell were because her program recommended:

- Choosing multiple-use products
- Selling at a profit-making price
- Offering an attractive package
- Giving the buyer a feeling of a real bargain
- Offering enough value so the sale "stuck"
- Making the customer happy

Susan's package of cloth flags (for the home) and paper flags (for the auto) were:

- Easy to mail
- Inexpensive to mail
- Reasonable in cost to her
- Low cost to the buyer

Get Started—Don't Waste Time

To obtain her mailing list at as low a cost as possible, Susan used local suburban telephone books. Her reasoning was:

- Most people in suburban phone books own their own homes
- Almost all home owners also own at least one car
- Home and auto owners are usually patriotic—they may buy flags

To test her theory, Susan addressed 1,000 envelopes herself and sent out a printed flyer (cost $6.50) advertising her flag package at $3.98. She received 200 orders. As each flag set cost her seventy cents, her gross profit worked out thus:

Gross income:	200 sets × $3.98	$796.00
Product cost:	$140.00	
Postage:	60.00	
Printing:	6.50	
Envelopes:	18.00	
Total cost:	224.50	
Gross profit:		$571.50

Since Susan "worked for fun," i.e., did not charge for her time, she had an excellent profit. But even if she had charged for the 25 hours she spent addressing the envelopes, she still would be in the chips.

Build Fast from Small Beginnings

Susan didn't waste time—she immediately expanded her list with an explosive zest. But it was then that she ran into a shortage of that delightful green stuff—money.

Using her ingenuity she combined handwriting analysis and body language to analyze the first bank loan officer she visited. Her analysis was so accurate that she obtained a loan for $5,000 within minutes.

Today, two years after her experimental start in mail order, Susan is selling more than 100 products ranging in price from $3.98 (her flag package) to $249.50 (a garden tool shed). Her annual income? A neat $140,000. That's a nice return for a small investment of time, money, and energy.

Pyramid Your Way to Wealth

Ralph L. needed $200,000 to start a plastics manufacturing business. Ralph had plenty of qualifications for the plastics business because he:

• Had worked in it for ten years
• Had studied the technology of plastics
• Had obtained several patents in the field

- Had an exact idea of what he wanted to market and sell

When Ralph L. came to me he had everything he needed to be a big success except one thing. And that, as you've probably guessed by now was a five-letter word—MONEY. "How," Ralph moaned, "can I raise two-hundred grand in a hurry? Particularly when I don't have a dime at the moment."

"Ralph, I'm on my way to Europe for a two-week lecture tour. So I can't help you at the moment. But if you do as I say, you can have the money you need within three days after I return."

"Great," he said enthusiastically. "What do I do?"

Here's what I had Ralph L. do. I call it my lucky 11-step mail-order road to *money*.

(1) Obtain six personal loan application forms from local banks or finance companies.

(2) Fill out each form—*neatly and clearly;* do not sign the form!

(3) Send each form by mail to the respective bank or finance company *on the same day;* ask for only *half* their maximum loan!

(4) Enclose a letter which says:
   (a) If I submitted this loan application this way, would you approve it?
   (b) What additional information is needed to have application approved?
   (c) How soon would I receive the loan I'm applying for?
   (d) How much money would you lend me?

(5) Sign all *approved* loan applications which the banks will mail to you after they've studied your letter and application. Then return the signed applications to the banks or finance companies.

(6) Deposit the checks received in a *savings account* to earn whatever interest you can until you decide what you'll do.

(7) Visit several local commercial banks and tell them

you're planning to open a *business checking account* in each bank.

(8) Ask the bank officer of each commercial bank how much of a loan he would grant you, using your borrowed money (but *don't* tell him it's *borrowed*) as a *compensating-balance.*

(9) Borrow the *full* loan the bank would make using a compensating-balance.

(10) Take the amount received from the loan and use it as a *second compensating-balance* deposit.

(11) Use the cash from the second compensating-balance loan to finance your business deal.

Put Your Plans into Action

Ralph swung into action while I was overseas on the trip I mentioned earlier. My European business lecture tour took me to London, Birmingham, Manchester, Stockholm, Hamburg, and Paris. Since I travel alone on these lecture tours, I thought about Ralph L. a great deal, wondering how he was doing. True, I was writing my money books on jets, in airport waiting areas, in hotel rooms, on trains, and even in taxis. As I tell people, you have to put your plans into action!

Within two hours after the big jet landed at JFK, the garage where I leave my car during these trips had delivered my Caddy to the International Arrivals Building and I had driven to my home town of Hicksville, N.Y., and tried to get some sleep. Then my business telephone began to ring. It was Ralph L.

"Ty, five of my six loans were approved!" he shouted with glee. "What do I do now?"

"Get your money," I said. "Did you do as I said and just ask for about half their maximum loan?"

"I did exactly as you advised," he replied. "And they all wanted to lend me more than I asked for! Can you believe it, Ty, these people were trying to throw money at me! I can pick up $3,000 from each bank, for a total of $15,000."

"Get it; then call me," I said.

Ralph L. got his $15,000—*all by mail.* He deposited this $15,000 in his business checking account and obtained a compensating-balance loan of five times this (the usual ratio) at his local commercial bank where he had deposited the $15,000. Taking this $75,000 to another bank, Ralph L. obtained a line of credit loan for five times this amount, or $375,000. Thus, Ralph L. expanded his capital from zero to $375,000 in less than three weeks!

"And where does handwriting analysis and body language come in?" you ask. In a number of places, including:

- Clear, neat preparation of the application forms
- Analysis of the loan officer's character from his signature on the letter replying to the questions
- Face-to-face body-language analysis of the loan officer when the application for the loan is given to him (if you give him the application in person)
- Awareness of how people unknowingly reveal their character traits in their handwriting and by their body movements and posture

Today Ralph L. has a flourishing plastics business and he has repaid *all* his loans. But just the other day he told me he's considering borrowing a million dollars to start another business. Once a wealth-builder, always a wealth-builder!

Take the Real-Estate Route to Wealth

Every major fortune ever built anywhere eventually includes some real estate. And many, many fortunes are built only on real estate. Why do people like real estate as a source of their fortune? Because real estate:

- Has solid, lasting value
- Appreciates quickly and surely
- Can be borrowed against—i.e., mortgaged
- May be held, built on, or developed
- Can be refinanced again and again

It was for these and other reasons that Bob C. wanted to build his fortune in real estate. But, like so many others, Bob was long on ambition, drive, and innovative ideas, but short on cash.

"Bob," I said when he came to me for advice, "I want you to find two or three pieces of property you like. Talk to the owners; get all the details on location, price, and potential increase in value. When you have this information we can sit down and see what the future holds."

Bob followed my recommendations and did as I said. Two weeks later he called. "Ty," he said excitedly, "I've found three pieces of ideal land. I want to stop over and tell you about them."

"Great! Hurry over."

Here's what Bob C. had come up with during his two-week search:

• Three pieces of prime growth-potential land
• One seller asking for only $100 down
• One seller seeking $10,000 down
• One seller seeking $5,000 down

Go First Class—All the Way

Analyzing the asking price and the potential appreciation value of the land we found that *the highest cost land had the greatest appreciation value!* This brings out an important principle, namely:

> A high-priced investment may have a larger potential appreciation than a low-cost investment. So don't buy on price alone—check out your potential profit before investing.

Now this is what I had Bob do:

(1) Write the owner of the $10,000-down property
(2) Ask him six questions about the land
(3) Ask for a *quick* response

Get the Facts You Need

What we hoped to obtain with the six questions was a reply from the land owner in his own handwriting. And that was exactly what we received. "Now, Bob," I said, "analyze this handwriting, or have it analyzed, to see what you can learn about the owner of this land." This is what Bob learned from the handwriting analysis—the landowner was:

- Difficult to get along with
- Interested in getting his own way
- A loud talker who tries to overpower people
- A person who might be careless in money matters
- Often impractical in business matters
- Arrogant, blustery, and given to strong opinions

We now had the facts we needed. These facts showed us that "our man" was a tough hombre. But once we knew this our dealings with him would be much easier because we knew him better than he knew himself. And all this was the result of handwriting analysis!

Plan Your Moves Carefully

Because we knew our man's basic personality traits, Bob planned to:

- Be as accommodating as possible
- Allow him to get his own way in unimportant matters
- Let him talk as much as he wanted
- Listen to his opinions

Using this approach, Bob was able to take over the land for a down payment of only $5,000, instead of the originally requested $10,000. And he borrowed the $5,000 from IWS Inc.! (Business loans are a service they offer to their subscribers.) Further, Bob was able to obtain the entire package of land—100 acres—for a total price of $30,000 or $300 per acre.

"Now I'll try to sell this land and see what happens," Bob laughed as he told me about the deal.

"Just hope and pray," I replied.

Buy Low—Sell High

Bob put the land up for sale and was soon offered $600 per acre. "What should I do?" he wailed. "Hold on," I advised. "The future is bright."

Several months later Bob called again. He was in a real tizzy. "Ty," he groaned, "the offering price is up to $1,000 an acre. And I'm afraid that if I don't sell now, the bottom will drop out of the land market."

"Never in your lifetime," I laughed. "Not with that beautiful piece of property you have—right on a main highway, smack in the way of the main line development. Hang on—you'll hit it big before you know it."

Bob sold out 18 months after he bought the land. His price? He sold the land for $3,000 per acre, giving him a selling price of $300,000. After deducting various expenses, including the cost of the land, interest on his loan, etc., Bob had a profit of $262,000 in just 18 months, using borrowed money to finance his land purchase!

Use Your Go-Power Now

Handwriting analysis—also called graphology—may not be your "thing" at the moment. But take a quick look at any of the books listed below on the subject and I'm sure you'll come up with some interesting findings which will pay off in your business.

And while you're looking at books on handwriting analysis, don't forget to glance at one or two books on body language. Combined with handwriting analysis, body language studies can really clue you in on a person's behavior in business.

Your modern *go-power* for *wealth-growing power* is here now. Use this power to put yourself into the big-money class today!

HELPFUL BOOKS ON HANDWRITING AND BODY LANGUAGE ANALYSIS

Brook—*Your Personality in Handwriting*, Associated Booksellers.
Bunker—*Handwriting Analysis*, Nelson-Hall.
Bunker—*What Handwriting Tells You*, Nelson-Hall.
Falcon—*How to Analyze Handwriting*, Simon & Schuster.
Fast—*Body Language*, M. Evans and Co., Inc.
Holder—*How Handwriting Analysis Can Improve Your Life*, Award Books.

Lucas—*Handwriting and Character Analysis*, Associated Booksellers.

Marcuse—*Guide to Personality Through Your Handwriting*, Arco.

Marley—*Handwriting Analysis Made Easy*, Borden.

Martin—*What Your Handwriting Reveals*, Meredith.

Mendel—*Personality in Handwriting*, Ungar.

Meyer—*Handwriting Analyzer*, Simon & Schuster.

Rand—*Graphology Handbook*, Wehman.

Rosen—*Science of Handwriting Analysis*, Crown.

Sara—*Complete Book of Handwriting Analysis for the Millions*, Dell.

Saudek—*Psychology of Handwriting*, Weiser.

ten

How to Build
Easy-Money Riches
Using Science

"What do you mean when you say I should use science to build wealth?" you ask. I have a ready answer because all my life I've used sciences of one kind or another to build wealth. Why limp along on uncertain facts, unclear assumptions, and unreliable data when, by using a little science, you can:

- Get the facts you need
- Make clearer, safer assumptions
- Develop reliable business data
- Arrive at accurate decisions

If I can use science in my wealth building, so can you because I'm no smarter than you are. In fact, you're probably smarter than I am because you have enough sense to read a book which will help you out. All I do is write these books!

Put Science to Work for Yourself Today

"What kinds of science should I put to work?" you ask. To answer your question as to what kinds of science you can use,

155

here are a few that can speed you on your way to wealth. When you're reading this list, please *don't be frightened by big or strange-sounding names!* The techniques I give you are easy and direct and, since they'll make you money, you'll love them. So consider using in your wealth-building activities:

- Statistics
- Averages
- Interest
- Samples
- Planning
- Budgeting

You may have other sciences you'd like to use. Great! My life has shown me, again and again, that:

> The more you think and plan in your business life, the greater your chances of success.

Use Statistics to Build Wealth

Many people call statistics *figures,* meaning numbers which are useful in making business decisions, such as:

- Should I buy this business?
- Will this business make me rich?
- How much does each customer spend in my business?
- What were the annual sales in this business last year?
- How much profit can I earn in this business?

You can obtain useful, profitable business statistics from numerous sources free of charge. These sources include:

- U.S. Government
- Your local library
- State industrial boards
- Chamber of Commerce

Put Your Statistics to Work

Typical business statistics you obtain will tell you many useful facts about a business you plan to enter. Here's how you can use such facts to:

(1) Decide what business you'd like to enter
(2) Determine the average income for this business
(3) Find out how many of these businesses are in operation locally, nationally, or internationally depending on the scope of your planned operations
(4) Determine the average number of employees in the business
(5) Determine the average profit in the business

With these statistics in hand you can decide if you want to go into the business you've been studying. Or you can look into other businesses which might prove more promising.

See How Others Do It

Richard M. always wanted to get into the rental real estate business. For years Richard dreamed of owning a string of apartment buildings and homes which he could rent to a large number of people. So Richard took Step 1, above, by writing down in a notebook the name of the business he wanted to enter—rental real estate.

Next, Richard called his local Real Estate Association on the telephone and told them of his interest in rental property. He asked the Association representative to send him any available data on local real-estate earnings and activities.

Within a few days Richard received a thick packet of information which quickly told him the:

• Average rental real-estate income in his area
• Number of rental real estate businesses in his local area
• Typical number of employees in the local rental businesses
• Average net operating profit of the local businesses

With this information in hand, Richard was ready to go to work. In building his fortune he used some of my famous financial formulas. Let's see how.

Be a Numbers Businessman

Every *numbers businessman* knows that, usually, on a statistical basis:

- There are more businesses for sale than there are buyers with money
- Sellers are *anxious;* buyers are *relaxed*
- Money is scarce; talk is cheap; promises are seldom kept
- An *anxious* seller will often finance you to your fortune

Knowing these facts about the usual selling situation, Richard planned to use them to build his fortune. Here's how.

(1) Select a suitable property, after careful inspection.

(2) Tell the owner you'd like to use the property as collateral for a loan for the cash down payment.

(3) Have the owner assign the property to you for a period long enough for you to get the loan (usually 60 days).

(4) Apply for the down-payment loan using the temporarily assigned property as collateral.

(5) Purchase the property using the borrowed money.

(6) Continue this procedure until you've obtained as many properties as you want.

Using these six magic formula steps to wealth, Richard took over 28 rental properties in his local area. Within sixteen months he raised his real-estate income from zero to $125,000 per year—all on borrowed money.

Don't Let Averages Fool You

Many people shun averages in their wealth-building program because they've heard so many stories of how some folks use averages to mislead or abuse people. Yet it just isn't true, at least for most averages, that they are misused. Instead, most averages can be powerful tools in your hands. I call averages one of my *magic money magnets* and I want to make them *your magic money magnets* as well. Let me show you how Clark M. uses money magnets.

Build Your Fortune in the Unusual

Clark M. wanted to go into the lamp business. He had all sorts of great ideas for truly creative lamp designs. While I'm not a lamp expert, I do like to see attractive lamps in my home. Clark's designs included cordless lamps (with rechargeable batteries) to get away from unattractive cords, ball-shaped lamps, birdcage lamps, etc. But Clark had one problem—he didn't have any money and there was a real squeeze on funds in the money market. "Clark," I said, "you have to find an unusual source of funds. And to do this I want you to consider using my magic money magnets—i.e., averages."

"I'll sure try," he laughed. Now here's what Clark did.

(1) Searched for unusual money sources
(2) Found the list of 2,500 overseas firms looking for American products listed in *Worldwide Riches Opportunities*
(3) Studied the needs of every firm in the list
(4) Found that some 300 firms—i.e., about one of every eight—were looking for lamps or lamp products
(5) Figured how much money he could borrow if an average of 100 firms each lent him an average of $100, $200, $300, etc.
(6) Checked to see if the money he thought he could obtain would be enough to put him in business
(7) Finding that he could probably borrow enough overseas to get started in the United States, Clark went ahead with his plans

Money Averages Pay Off

Clark studied his numbers again and decided that the average loan he probably could obtain would be $350. Also, he estimated that he could get a loan of this amount from 100 of the 300 firms interested in lamps. This would give him a total capital of $350 × 100 = $35,000 to start his lamp business.

Next Clark formed a company and had a letterhead printed using his home address. The total cost of these two steps was $56. With everything ready to go, Clark then prepared, and had printed, sketches and short descriptions of his lamps. Then he sat down and typed letters himself to each of the 300 companies he had selected as loan candidates. He included with the letter some reproductions of his lamp sketches and descriptions.

Clark soon found that his estimates based on the magic money magnet he had developed were wrong. Instead of each firm lending him an average of $350, the average worked out to $752—say $750 for talking purposes. And instead of an average of 100 firms lending him $35,000, only 71 advanced money, giving him a total loan of 71 × 752 = $53,392! Hence he beat his goal by $18,392. That's a nice plus to start business with!

Clark's loan was more than he needed to get started. Today Clark has a booming lamp business (more than $1 million per year) with many customers in both the United States and overseas. Yet he got his start by using an unusual *magic money magnet*.

Wheel and Deal Your Way to Wealth

There are thousands of would-be wheelers and dealers—people who'd like to be big shots in the *big* money arena—in the world today. Yet my experiences in almost every country in the world show that a wheeler-dealer can only hit the big money if he has the *inside* track on key information, such as:

- Sources of 100% financing for business deals
- Finder's fee offers and opportunities
- Free business help
- Clear guidance for becoming a financial broker, finder, business broker, and business consultant
- Thousands of import-export opportunities
- Lists of top executive search firms
- Instant millionaire guides and techniques

To obtain such inside information, many wheeler-dealers subscribe to, and regularly read, *International Wealth Success,* the beginning and experienced wealth-builder's monthly newsletter which costs $24 per year. If you'd like to wheel and deal in your business activities by using this helpful newsletter, send $24 to IWS Inc., P.O. Box 186, Merrick, N.Y. 11566. You'll be glad you did.

How Wheeler-Dealers Work

A wheeler-dealer is a person who takes maximum advantage of the opportunities available to him for earning a large fortune, including:

- 100% financing
- Advantageous tax laws and tax shelters
- Other people's money
- Fast writeoffs of assets
- Sale and leaseback arrangements

The wheeler-dealer is completely honest—he neither breaks the law nor bends it. But the wheeler-dealer often:

- Works fast
- Slashes through red tape
- Makes every moment count
- Seldom invests a penny of his own money
- Jumps from deal to deal, pyramiding wealth as he goes
- Seeks to build wealth speedily, instead of waiting a lifetime
- Spots wealth opportunities before others do

Work the Way Wheeler-Dealers Do

Chris B. lives on the West Coast of the United States, right in the middle of the aerospace manufacturing area. Several years ago, when cutbacks in government contracts led to mass layoffs of aerospace workers, Chris B. started to wheel and deal. He's been doing it profitably every since.

Many of the laid-off workers decided to move from the West

Coast to other areas to find new jobs. This caused a large number of homes to be offered for sale, driving down the prices of homes in the area. As the prices of homes decreased, so did the required cash down payment.

"I have faith in this area," Chris recalls. "Though we were in a minor depression of home prices, I knew that business would return to the aerospace industry and we'd have a shortage of homes, instead of a surplus. Also, I figured the average price I'd have to pay for a home, and the average cash I'd get from selling a home."

Chris bought ten houses, using money he borrowed from the bank on personal loans as the cash down payment. To help make the mortgage payments, Chris rented the houses to needy local families. Six months later when new contracts were given to aerospace and defense firms in the area, a housing shortage developed as new workers moved into the area. Chris, with his ten houses ready for sale, had no trouble selling them at an excellent profit. And he's been doing it ever since, whenever business or other conditions cause homes to come on the market at low prices.

Note these features about this example of wheeling and dealing:

- Spotting a trend (low price houses)
- Figuring the averages
- Holding the item for a short time
- Selling at a profit
- Seeking new deals

You can do the same. Just use the above steps as your guide to an enormous profit as a wheeler-dealer.

Know the Ins and Outs of Interest

Interest which we pay, or is paid to us, has several unique characteristics which, as fortune builders, we should keep in mind. Thus, interest is:

- Tax deductible when paid
- Taxable when received
- An extra cost to us when we borrow
- Income to us when we lend

Since most of us *pay* interest on the money we borrow, we'll devote more space to that aspect of interest than to any other.

To make money on borrowed money, or as many wealth-builders say, on OPM, *Other People's Money*:

The income we receive from the investment of OPM must exceed all the expenses of the investment, including interest.

Let me give you an example from a real-life business which a friend of mine runs.

Put OPM to Work for Yourself

Ted C. borrowed a total of $25,000 from several lenders to buy a small manufacturing business. He found the lenders listed in the book *Business Capital Sources,* available for $15.00 from IWS Inc., P.O. Box 186, Merrick, N.Y. 11566. Since Ted's credit rating wasn't superlative, he had to borrow from more than one lender and the book gave him exactly what he needed—lists of hundreds and hundreds of organizations and people ready to lend money in amounts ranging from $500 to $50 million. Now let's see how Ted arranged his financial life to earn a big income.

The expenses of Ted's business worked out thus:

Expense	$ per year
Labor	$24,000
Materials	8,000
Rent	3,000
Utilities	1,000
Other	1,000
Total	$37,000

The income earned by the business was:

Product	Income $ per year
Manufactured items	$62,000
Salvage of raw materials	3,000
Commissions and miscellaneous	1,000
Total	$66,000

The difference between the income and expenses, or $66,000 — $37,000 = $29,000 is what Ted has available to pay off his $25,000 debt, the interest on this debt, any remaining debts on the business, and the interest on those debts. Here's how it worked for Ted.

Price of business	$100,000	
Down payment	25,000	
Balance due	$ 75,000	
Annual net income	$ 29,000	
Annual debt repayment including interest		
On $25,000 loan	$ 6,000	(5 years)
On $75,000 loan	$ 9,000	(10 years)
Total annual debt repayment	$ 15,000	
Cash "throw"	$ 14,000	

Hence, Ted had an annual income of $14,000 while the:

* Business was paying for itself
* Interest payments were combined with the loan re-payments
* Business ran itself

Within two years Ted had tripled the business income—and his own income. Yet this was a second-income or moonlighting business for Ted. And what made it a success? There are several factors, including:

* Combining the interest and loan repayments for easier handling
* Having a ready source of funds from *Business Capital Sources*
* Using 100% financing to buy the business
* Wise tax planning to take advantage of legitimate interest, depreciation, and non-competitive covenant deductions

As Ted says, "Why moonlight at low hourly wages where the taxes kill you, when with a little help from the newsletter *International Wealth Success,* and its various courses and books, you can hit the big money quickly and easily?"

Use Random Samples to Get Fast Data

As some of my readers know, I'm a busy guy because besides writing books in my spare-spare time, I'm:

- President of a multi-million-dollar lending and financial organization
- An executive in a firm on *Fortune* magazine's list of the 500 largest corporations in the United States
- A worldwide lecturer
- An international consultant
- President of two successful growing corporations
- Owner of a number of highly successful mail-order products

"Why are you beating your chest this way, Mr. Author?" you ask. To which I reply, "I'm *not* beating my chest, I'm just trying to show you that I'm qualified by long *actual* experience to advise you on how to make a big bundle of money. And one way to get started is by using random samples."

And what's a *random sample?* A random sample is an observation, reading, count, or other measure taken at unplanned intervals. Because the sample is unplanned, i.e., random, you can obtain an amazing degree of accuracy using nothing more than your eyes, ears, a pencil, and paper. Let's see how.

Make a Million by Investing Only Your Time

Let's say you want to buy a going business (which I strongly recommend over opening a new business). The business you like is a sea food restaurant perched on a cliff overlooking the beautiful blue Pacific south of Los Angeles and out of the smog belt. You know something about the food side of restaurants but you are somewhat doubtful about the income this restaurant might develop for you.

How can you *accurately* and *economically* check out this potential deal? That's easy. Use random samples. Here's what you could do.

(1) Determine the hours the business is open (say noon to 1:00 a.m.)

(2) Figure the average bill per customer (using the menu, you figure the average bill as $6.50, including drinks)

(3) Visit, and count the number of customers patronizing the business, at *random* times during the day and night

(4) Compute the income the customers being served would generate for your business

Now what do I mean by *random* times? Just this. If your first visit of the day is 1:00 p.m., your next visit might be at 2:30 p.m., the next 3:00 p.m. Thus, you *do not* observe every hour, every half hour, etc. You observe at *random* intervals. Thus, the first observation might be on the hour; the next on the half hour, etc. Note this fact:

> The randomness of your observations provides the statistical accuracy you seek.

Let's say that your random observations quickly show you that the business is generating an average income of $2,100 per week. Since the seller has already told you that he is reporting an income of about $100,000 per year, you have quickly verified his statement by using simple statistics. (You can obtain a second verification by examining his business income tax returns for the last several years.)

Knowing these facts about the business, and after having examined the tax returns of the business for previous years, you buy the business. You quickly build it to a level where you can buy another business. Soon your income and net worth are building toward that magic million-dollar mark. And all because you spent a little time in applying science to your business!

If you really want to explore business arithmetic more deeply, take a look at one or more of the books on this subject listed at the end of this chapter. You may find this subject both interesting and rewarding.

Plan Your Way to Wealth

You probably watch TV now and then. If you ever watch some of the mystery thrillers you may notice that some of the private detectives appear to solve their crimes after doing little advance planning. Such an approach might work on the color TV screen but it will fail in real life.

To make big money you *must* plan every move from:

> • Choice of your business
> • Price to pay for the business
> • Operating methods
> • Taxes you'll pay
> • Selling price when you're ready to sell the business
> • Selling-price pay out to you in the future.

Planning is work—that's why most people avoid plans whenever they can. Yet one minute spent in planning can pay big dividends for years and years.

To plan your way to the big money, take these steps:

(1) *Decide* what you want—for instance an income of $100,000 per year.
(2) *Select* a way to achieve your goal—pick the business or job you like.
(3) *Plan* each step you'll take on your way to your goal by preparing a numbered list of the steps you'll take.
(4) *Assign* a completion date to each step—i.e., make a schedule.
(5) *Start* working on your wealth plan.
(6) *Compare* your actual progress with your planned progress.
(7) *Act* to reduce any falling behind in your planned schedule.
(8) *Work* to make your plan work.

How Plans Pay Off

To show you how plans can pay off, I have to tell you a story about myself. As president of a multi-million dollar loan and financial organization, I ride to work from my home to New York City on the Long Island Railroad. On this train I often worry about how we can get more people to borrow money from us.

One dreary morning I was sitting on the train in Jamaica

station staring out into the dull gray rain. I had finished my daily worry about trying to find more lenders, and was wondering how I could *select* a mail-order item that would earn me a million dollars in my spare time. That is, I wanted to "moonlight." I had earlier *decided* on mail order instead of some franchise involving cooking, auto repair, equipment leasing, etc. Why mail order? Because I:

- Enjoy working at home
- Like the freedom mail order offers
- Love to receive mail
- Get pleasure from working with the post office
- See a big future for mail order

As I was sitting there staring into the rain I began to think of the big mail-order successes—Sears, Montgomery Ward, International Correspondence Schools, National Radio Institute—and how they had scored big. What I didn't realize at the time was that my mind was seeking, for me, a *similar* success which I could select.

Suddenly my mind seemed to reach out and surround an idea. Why not start a mail-order school for training wealth-builders? After all, there are schools for house builders, electronics equipment builders, etc. Wealth-builders are entitled to a school, also.

So, having *decided* on mail order, I *selected* the way to achieve my goal. Next came *planning, assigning* dates, *starting* work, *comparing* actual vs. planned progress, *acting* to keep on schedule, and *working* to make my plan work.

The rest of this story is history. I started the *Instant-Millionaire Fortune Builders Program* to train people by mail on how to build a big fortune quickly. The *program* caught on quickly because it is:

- A self-study type—no homework is required
- Practical procedures are featured
- Anyone interested in making *big* money can use the data given
- The cost is low

- Membership in the Fortune Builders Club is included in the price

After offering the *Instant-Millionaire Fortune Builders Program* for a few years I turned it over to IWS Inc., Box 186, Merrick, N.Y. 11566, because other interests were taking up too much of my time. Priced at $99.50, this *program* is a great bargain for anyone interested in quick wealth building.

Budget Your Way to Great Wealth

When we hear the word *budget,* most of us think of the famous household budget used by young marrieds to control their spending. Such budgets are good, of course. But just as important are business budgets. Yet many beginning wealth-builders —and even experienced ones—somehow think they can run a successful business *without* a budget. Let me tell you one fact I've learned over the years:

> You can seldom make really *big* money in business without careful budgeting and planning. These are the two financial keys to great success in any business.

So don't turn your back on budgeting, particularly when this approach may put you in the big money within months.

Just what is a budget in business? The answer is simple:

A budget is a financial plan. And a plan, in turn, is a business objective you intend to achieve during a specified time period.

Typical business objectives include:

- Sales of $X at a cost of $Y
- A profit of Z% on sales

When you budget for business purposes you:

- Select your business objectives—such as sales in dollars and units
- Estimate the cost of achieving these objectives

- Budget the estimated costs by spreading them over a time period—usually one year
- Compare actual costs with planned or budgeted costs as you work toward your goals

Keep Budgets Simple

A friend of mine runs a $10 million business from which he takes home a salary of $375,000 a year. Yet his annual budget for this business is so simple that he keeps it on one side of one sheet of 8½ × 11 inch paper. He carries his budget with him wherever he goes because it doesn't weigh him down at all.

You can do the same for your business. To learn the effectiveness of budgeting from your own firsthand experience, just try using a budget for a few weeks in your personal finances. You'll be amazed at the accuracy you can obtain when you make simple estimates and forecasts, and then exert control over your money.

Then apply budgeting to your business activities and you'll soon see your fortune growing. Why miss out when you, too, can be one of the wealthy people of this world? Try budgeting and see. It will cost you nothing but pencil and paper. And if you have trouble preparing your *business* budget, see an accountant in your local area. He'll be delighted to help you because you're starting out right! Make full use of your accountant.

Make Science Pay Off for You

In this chapter we've shown you a few scientific aids that can make you wealthy in just a few months. Put these *aids* to work now and you may soon become the world's fastest wealth-builder. Use my methods because they are:

- Proven
- Practical
- Profitable

Could you ask for any more from a good friend?

USEFUL BOOKS ON BUSINESS FIGURING

Battersby—*Mathematics in Management*, Pelican
Candee—*Business Facts of Business Arithmetic*, Collier
Curry—*Basic Mathematics for Business Analysis*, Irwin
Feldman—*Mathematics of Business Affairs*, Allyn & Bacon
Golde—*Thinking with Figures in Business*, Addison-Wesley
Huffman—*Arithmetic for Business and Consumer Use*, McGraw-
Hill
Lowenstein—*Mathematics in Business*, Wiley
Minrath—*Handbook of Business Mathematics*, Van Nostrand
Neinstein—*Business Arithmetic*, Barron's

eleven

How to Figure
Your Best
Money-Making Days

In <u>my previous money-making books</u>,* I emphasized the many legal and business aspects of getting rich in a hurry. The present book covers, in addition to numerous legal and business topics, many of the important *mind* topics related to accumulating wealth.

What is the reason for this emphasis on the mind in this book? Because:

You can think yourself rich! Plenty of people do it every day of the year. Likewise, you can think yourself poor.

I want you to think yourself rich, not poor! So this book gives you the mind approach to building fast riches.

---

* *How to Build a Second-Income Fortune in Your Spare Time; Smart Money Shortcuts to Becoming Rich; How to Start Your Own Business on a Shoestring and Make up to $100,000 a Year; How to Borrow Your Way to a Great Fortune,* all published by Parker Publishing Co, Inc., West Nyack, N.Y. 10994.

Work Your Mind and Body

You are familiar, I'm sure with the usual "ups and downs" most of us experience in our daily lives. Some people describe these ups and downs as *good days* and *bad days*. On a good day:

- Your mind is extra sharp
- Your body feels good all over
- You could climb the highest mountain
- Business deals are easy to swing

But on a bad day:

- You feel tired
- Your mind is dull
- You want to relax—get away from it all
- You "couldn't care less" about business

With such wide ranges in our feelings and interests, we'd be wiser if we knew when to expect our good and bad days. Many of the most successful wealth-builders I know take special steps to find out exactly when to expect their good and bad days. Knowing in advance when they'll be mentally and physically sharp helps these outstandingly successful wealth-builders pick their best days for profitable business deals.

You can do the same—i.e., determine your good and bad days—if you want to. And if you do, your cost will be zero, if you exclude the cost of a sheet of paper and pencil. Knowing which are your good and bad days might mean the difference between success and failure in a big, important business deal.

Three Who Hit It Big

Here are three capsule stories of people, just like yourself, who hit the big money quickly. Part of their success came from knowing their good and bad days.

HOME FIRE ALARMS

In three years Bill S. built a $10 million-per-year business from scratch. Starting by working out of his apartment, he sold home fire alarms. Today he has some 3,000 salesmen working for him, rides in his company jet plane, and drives the best of cars. Yet three years ago he was a door-to-door salesman of pots and pans! How did Bill get so rich so fast? By figuring his good and bad days and selling hardest on his good days. On his bad days he planned his sales tactics for his good days, which he knew would return soon.

LIFE INSURANCE PAYS OFF

When people hear of a life-insurance man who made it big they usually think of the salesman who's a member of the Million-Dollar Club. But Frank B. hit the big money fast in life insurance a different way—he founded his own company and hired salesmen to sell his product—life insurance. Today he has more than $300 million of insurance in force, yet he started only two years ago! "I started on a good day," Frank confides. "And almost every day since then has been a good one for me! On a bad day I play golf or go fishing. I've learned to figure out my money-making days."

MAKE LAND PAY OFF

A friend of mine, Joel C. is in the marine canvas business— he makes Navy tops, hull covers, and similar products for boats of all sizes. During the past eight years, Joel has been working hard to earn as much as possible in his canvas business. During the same time he's been paying off the corner one-story brick building in which he runs his business. The day he made his last payment on his building a representative of a big real-estate company came along and offered Joel an enormous price for his building. "I was amazed," Joel said. "The profit I'd earn on the sale of my building would average three times the usual annual profit from the marine canvas business and the income tax rate on the sale of my building would be lower than on the business! Boy, did I learn from this deal." What Joel means is that *a real-estate using business often profits more from the sale of real estate than from the sale of the business products, if the real estate location is good.* This fact reinforces the concept that there are *three* principles to making money in real estate—and only three—(1) Location, (2) Location, (3) Location!

Find Your Best Days

You can find your best days in a number of ways, including:

(1) Keeping simple daily readings of your moods in a dated diary
(2) Using the biorhythm system
(3) Asking others to tell you your mood

Once you know if a given day is a *good* or *bad* day for you, you can take any necessary steps to prevent over-enthusiasm or low spirits from causing trouble in your business or personal life.

Keep a Record of Your Moods

Most of us have a distinct pattern to our moods. We all know that on some days we're "high"—i.e., we feel good and our mental attitude is positive with all signals *go*. Yet a few days later we may feel depressed, discouraged, and lost.

Keep a record of your moods on a form such as the Mood Cycle Analyzer on page 185 and you'll soon see a pattern emerging from day to day, week to week, and month to month. Thus, you might find that for twelve days around the middle of the month you feel great, your brain is sharp, and you're always ready for action. If so, these days are good for you and your business deals.

Leading up to your twelve "high" days you might have eight days of increasingly good feelings. And following your twelve "high" days you might have ten days of decreasing enthusiasm and drive. Thus, your mood cycle might repeat itself every thirty days or so during the year.

Not everyone has a thirty-day cycle. You might have a twenty-day cycle, or some other interval. Much depends on yourself and the way you live. But remember these facts about mood cycles:

• There's no such thing as a "perfect" cycle
• You're you, and *your* cycle is unique to *you*
• Cycles may vary slightly from month to month

- Knowing your mood cycle *can* put money in your pocket
- *Not knowing* your mood cycle can rob money from your pocket

Moods Can Pay Off

If you could spend a few weeks with me visiting and talking to budding millionaires all over the world, you'd quickly see that:

- You can make money from *positive* moods
- *Negative* moods can be turned to positive moods
- You can build a fortune anywhere, any time—if you work hard

Marty L. found this out recently after talking to me about building a fortune in a hurry. "Gee, I wish I could make as much money as you do," Marty said during our first meeting. "That's easy," I laughed. "Just put in as many hours as I do, and work as hard as I do, and you'll probably earn more!"

To show Marty that he could really build a fortune quickly, I took him to see a highly successful friend of mine. We took a bus from midtown New York City to a town in New Jersey to visit this friend. As soon as we boarded the bus I took out a pad of paper and began writing. "What are *you* doing?" Marty asked in a slightly peevish tone. "I'm working, Marty. I work everywhere because a thought here and a thought there soon adds up to a book, an article, or even a speech. And each of these means money to me, Marty."

In the lobby of my friend's factory we had to wait for about twenty minutes. I started working again while Marty sat and twiddled his thumbs while staring at the ceiling. Once inside the factory, Marty was treated to another eye-opener. My friend proudly showed us around his neat, modern factory.

In his office, which was beautifully furnished, there was a closed door alongside the desk. "What's that door for?" Marty asked. "That's my mini-apartment, where I stay when I work late on one of my good days," my friend replied. "I make my moods pay off by working longer hours on good days."

I could see Marty's eyes widen. In the last two hours he'd had two clear and specific examples of making moods pay off—my friend (whose success was obvious), and myself (whose success is widely known). Both of us could trace our riches, in part at least, to seizing the mood of the moment and turning it into business success.

Make Your Moods Your Money-Magic

Your good days can yield riches beyond your most fervent dreams if you make your moods your money-magic. What do I mean by money-magic? Just this:

When you make your moods money-magic you convert a feeling (happy or unhappy) into a wealth-building force which can put money into your pocket.

The main point to keep in mind is the *conversion* of a mood into positive action. Let me give you an example.

My friend Marty remarked, after the visit I described above, that his best moods often came at night when he was in bed and fully rested. Not only did he feel good at that time, he also had his best ideas then. "I'll have to think of a way to jot these ideas down so I'll remember them in the morning," Marty said.

Two weeks later Marty called, full of excitement. "I had a great idea last night and I was able to trap it by jotting it down on my bedside 'mood pad,'" he said.

Marty's idea was to print, and distribute, a collection of industrial catalogs for specialized industries. The manufacturers would supply the catalogs free and would pay a fee for having their material included in the master file which would be a large bound book about four inches thick. Users of the catalog would also pay a fee for their copy of the catalog which would be sent to them once a year.

Marty started his catalog service with a capital of only $500. Today, four years later his business is grossing $3 million per year. All because Marty:

- Became sensitive to his moods by keeping a record of them
- Trapped his good-mood ideas
- Took action to put his good-mood ideas to work

In single-word summaries of your mood use, you can say that you must:

- Know (what your mood is)
- Capture (your good ideas)
- Act (on your good ideas)

Apply this KCA (Know, Capture, Act) approach to *your* wealth search and you can't go wrong. For when you *know* your moods, when you *capture* the good ideas springing from these moods, and when you *act* on these ideas you have an unbeatable combination.

Try Biorhythm in Your Wealth Search

Biorhythm, developed and perfected in Europe by Dr. William Fliess, is an outgrowth of centuries of observation of man by himself. Thus, as far back as Hippocrates, the Greek medical doctor, mention was made of man's *good* and *bad* days. And even Goethe, the German poet, mentions in his personal writings these kinds of days.

Biorhythm, then is the study and prediction of our moods and physical condition and the cycles they follow. For you, or any other individual, biorhythm classifies your moods and physical condition and the cycles they follow, under three categories:

- Sensitive—i.e., your over-all mood
- Intellectual—i.e., your mental ability at a given time
- Physical—i.e., the energy we have to get things done

Knowing these three cycles for ourselves, we can determine, in advance, whether we should be careful in a given business deal which requires a:

- Sensitivity to the feelings of others
- Rigorous mental analysis
- Concentrated physical effort

Thus, biorhythm *won't* solve your business problems for you. But it *will* tell you which areas of your personality require extra attention when you start a deal and work on it.

Plot Your Biorhythm

You can plot your biorhythm on a horizontal time scale. To make the plot you use three curves, one for sensitivity, one for your intellectual mood, and one for your physical condition. By studying the three curves you can easily determine your over-all condition with respect to both your business and personal life.

For complete details on biorhythm and its uses, I suggest you read a copy of *Biorhythm* by H. J. Wernli, Crown Publishers, Inc. This short, concise book quickly shows you how to apply the techniques of biorhythm in both your personal and business life.

Have Your Friends Help You

The author of this book is—as you know—your *good* friend. Others may let you down, but *your* author always comes through for you! You can depend on him. (Sometimes when things are a trifle rushed he may be delayed a little, but just be patient.)

If you have other friends—and I most certainly hope that you do—you can ask them to keep track of your moods on a day-to-day basis. To get the best results from such a deal, volunteer to keep track of your friend's moods too. Then you'll all work harder and develop more accurate results.

Mitch K. kept records of his friends' moods while they kept records of his. It didn't take Mitch long to learn, from these records, that he was often in a vile mood, as his friends described it. Further, Mitch learned that he tended to be:

- Cranky and short-tempered
- Sarcastic and insulting
- Impatient with, and insensitive to others
- Loud and argumentative

Despite these characteristics, Mitch K. had numerous acquaintances and a few good friends. Prior to the mood record-keeping, Mitch had been thinking of going into the public relations business by opening his own agency. But the reports of his friends clearly indicated to Mitch that the less contact he had with the public the fewer people he would offend. So Mitch decided to find a business in which he'd have the minimum contact with the public.

Mitch enjoyed reading books about success and similar subjects. Some of the books Mitch read were old, but the principles were still valid. One day, while mulling over what he should do, Mitch wondered if he could sell success books by mail order. When he mentioned his idea to me, my answer was a quick and short "You'll never know until you try!"

Here's what Mitch did to try out his idea of selling success books by mail order.

- Prepared a list of books and a two-line description of each
- Had the list, an order blank, and a return envelope printed
- Mailed 100 copies of the list to names selected from various telephone books
- Kept a careful record of the orders received
- Extended the mailing to 200 more names when he saw that the list would pay off:
- Continued extending the list, keeping a careful record of the results he was obtaining

Within a month Mitch was in the mail-order business. To strengthen his knowledge of mail order, Mitch took a course on the subject from IWS, Inc., P.O. Box 186, Merrick, New York 11566. Costing $99.50, this quick but complete course in mail order called *100 Easy Ways to Great Mail Order Success*, showed Mitch how to:

- Pick mail-order products
- Put the best price on a product
- Find low-cost mailing lists
- Prepare promotion materials
- Make a mailing
- Evaluate the response to the mailing
- Extend a mailing
- Predict results of additional mailings
- Compute product profit
- Plus many other practical, hard-hitting techniques

In his first month in business Mitch invested $400, including the cost of his course from IWS. His gross income that month was $837. Here's how Mitch did for the remainder of his first year:

Month	Cost	Income	Profit
2nd	$612	$1,317	$705
3rd	841	1,723	882
4th	1,605	3,307	1,702
5th	2,118	4,006	1,888
6th	2,531	5,692	3,161
7th	3,008	6,125	3,117
8th	3,534	7,219	3,785
9th	4,061	8,307	4,246
10th	4,509	9,223	4,714
11th	5,610	10,808	5,198
12th	6,150	13,543	7,393

Today, a year later, Mitch is grossing $200,000 a year in his mail-order business. And he gives as the keys to his success two factors:

- Knowing about his difficult personality, based on the analysis of his moods by his friends
- Accurate and practical mail-order procedures obtained from a well-prepared mail-order study course

Move Ahead to Great Wealth

Many advisers to Beginning Wealth-Builders (BWBs) assume that the beginner can easily put his hands on at least $5,000 cash. Yet my experience with thousands of BWBs shows that hardly any of the people I meet can put their hands on even $500 cash. Now I don't mean to be offensive—I'm just telling it as it is in *my* world. That's why I always try my ICFY—*Instant Cash For You*—approach to every BWB I advise who is short of cash. (And, good friends, most are!)

Using the ICFY approach you:

- Find *instant* cash
- Start earning *big* money fast
- Take up to *seven years* to repay
- Pyramid your way to greater *wealth*

- *Leverage* yourself to new, instant fortunes
- *Diversify* to marvelous security

Make Instant Cash Yours by Mail

"What do you mean by *instant cash?*" you ask. "And by mail, yet!"

By instant cash by mail I mean:

- Borrowed money, i.e., other people's money, obtained by *not* showing up in person for an interview
- Obtained by mail
- Sent to you by registered mail
- Received by you as a certified check
- Loaned to you within *seven days* after your application is received
- Positive Yes or No answer given by phone within 24 hours after your application is received

Now if a 24-hour positive yes or no answer and money within seven days through the mail doesn't seem like *instant cash* to you, let me give you a few facts of money life:

- No lender can give you an answer in *less than 24 hours*
- *It is almost impossible* to get cash into your hands in less than seven days when you borrow by mail
- There are very few mail-order loan agencies—and most of them won't lend you more than $2,000 for more than 24 months
- Yet the organization I'm about to tell you about will lend up to $500,000 per deal for up to seven years with a balloon repayment plan

If $500,000 in cash and a seven-year term for your loan is unsuitable for you because the:

- Amount is too small
- Repayment period is too short

then I can't help you as much as I'd like to in this paragraph. But just stay around and we'll help you in a moment.

To obtain *instant cash* in amounts up to $500,000 for periods up to seven years, subscribe for two years to *International Wealth Success*, P.O. Box 186, Merrick, N.Y. 11566. When you send your $48 subscription fee for this helpful and creative monthly newsletter, ask for their *business* loan application. When you receive the application, fill it out and send it to IWS. You will have your response within a few days, or by telephone, if you wish, within 24 hours. And, if IWS can't lend you the money you need, they'll tell you where you can borrow it.

If you need more than $500,000 for business purposes, buy a copy of *Business Capital Sources* for $15 from IWS at the above address. This useful book lists hundreds and hundreds of banks, finance companies, and private lenders willing to lend amounts up to $50 million, or more. But with some of these lenders, when you want to borrow more than $500,000 you must expect:

- A *full* credit investigation
- Possible delays
- Requests for collateral and cosigners
- Reams of paperwork

However, even these problems are minor, compared to being completely without money! So why not get double coverage—subscribe to the newsletter and buy the book. Then you'll have the best of both worlds!

Never Neglect Your Moods

Remember—*you are you*. And in the world of business:

Your moods are unique. By knowing your mood every day of the year, you are better prepared to win the business battle!

Self-knowledge is the most difficult kind of knowledge to obtain. But by focussing on your moods you can become:

- More successful
- Wiser, more mature
- A better negotiator
- An inspired wealth-builder

So start studying your moods today. You may even learn to like yourself better! After all, who can be nicer to you than yourself?

MY MOOD CYCLE ANALYZER

Day of Month	Physical Mood			Mental Mood		
	Excellent	Fair	Poor	Excellent	Fair	Poor
1						
2						
3						
4						
5						
6						
7						
8						
9						
10						
11						
12						
13						
14						
15						
16						
17						
18						
19						
20						
21						
22						
23						
24						
25						
26						
27						
28						
29						
30						
31						

To use this Analyzer, check off each day your *Physical Mood* (i.e., how you feel in terms of your health), and your *Mental Mood* (i.e., how you feel in terms of your mind). By drawing a line which connects the check marks you can obtain a graph of your mood cycle for the month. Keep a record of your moods for a year and you'll soon see how your moods affect your fortune building success.

twelve

Putting Psychic
Power to Work
in Your Money Life

Wealth-builders come in all sizes—tall, short, lean, and stout. And these same wealth-builders use all sorts of methods to:

- Guide their business actions
- Glean useful information
- Analyze people
- Plan future strategy
- Explain mistakes

And since this book is designed to tell you as much as possible about the various methods people use to build wealth, I'm devoting this chapter to an important technique termed *psychic money power.*

Understand Psychic Money Power

The usual definition of the word *psychic* is that it covers mental—i.e., non-physical—phenomena of any type. And *psychic money power* is the use of these mental skills to analyze business situations so you earn more money, faster.

And just what might psychic money power do for you in your wealth-building activities? Well it might:

- Help you understand people better
- Allow you to master people and situations
- Show you how to see the future more clearly
- Help you build wealth faster

Develop Your Psychic Money Powers

Is everyone born psychic? No, I don't think so. But you can become more psychic than you are now, simply by working at it. For just like any other part of the body, the mind becomes less effective when it isn't used regularly and vigorously.

To develop *your* psychic money power (PMP) take these steps:

(1) Read this chapter carefully.
(2) In every business and personal situation, try to "read" the thoughts and intentions of the other person.
(3) Keep a simple record of your score in each situation— showing if your psychic money powers are working well.
(4) Continue developing your psychic money power until you have mastered this skill.

Henry R. Luce, founder of one of the world's largest publishing firms, Time-Life, Inc., said, "Business, more than any other occupation, is a continual dealing with the future; it is a continual calculation, an instinctive exercise in foresight."

Thus, whatever means *you* use to improve your dealing with the future, you will increase your profit potential, if you can keep your foresight accurate.

Three Who Mastered Psychic Money Powers

Ken B. wanted to hit the *big* money more than anything else in life. One day Ken was offered the chance to go into the retail hardware business. To take advantage of this "golden" chance, Ken had to come up with $30,000 in cash. Since he didn't have a spare dime, this meant that Ken would have to borrow the money.

Using the IWS book *Business Capital Sources,* Ken easily and quickly found a lender ready to make a $30,000 loan for 84 months. With the money "in his hand," Ken felt less pressure to make a decision. So he sat down to think things over. Ken's budding psychic money powers immediately showed him that:

- Profits in the retail hardware business are low— usually only 5%.
- Suppliers can hurt you with late deliveries, short discounts, and high prices.
- A 5% profit potential is an extremely small reward for risking $30,000 of other people's money (OPM).
- The lower the potential profit percentage, the greater the risk of failure.

Thus, Ken "saw" in his mind's eye the drawbacks of this retail hardware business. Based on his psychic findings, Ken decided not to invest the money.

Later, after more study, Ken invested in a low-overhead mail-order publishing business and today is a millionaire. "Mail order has always offered higher profit margins than retail hardware," Ken says with a smile. "And my psychic money powers really work in mail order!" To round out Ken's story, let me tell you about two other psychic successes.

See Your Future Riches

Rose T. is an attractive, intelligent widow. She enjoys working with children and dreaming up new toys for them. These toys are so popular with the kids that many of Rose's friends tell her: "Rosie, you're so clever, you should go into the business!"

Rose, who's had psychic experiences in the past, decided to apply her "seeability" to the toy business. This is what she found:

- Toys, when successful, can bring enormous *riches.*
- Toys, when failures, can bring enormous *losses.*
- There's no way of knowing, in advance, which toys will fail, and which will win.
- To be successful in any business, you *must* take risks.

Rose continued her psychic exploration of the business world. To her delight she began to see that:

- Success is reachable by those who try
- Money snowballs as one success builds on another success
- You don't need "connections" if you have drive
- All the world loves a winner
- Anyone can earn *big, big money*

Once she had these facts clearly in mind (as the result of her psychic money power thinking), Rose was ready to move ahead. And move she did.

Corner a Profitable Idea

Knowing toys and kids, Rose decided that she wanted to go into the toy business *without*:

- Buying or leasing a factory
- Investing in machinery
- Hiring a big labor force
- Ordering carloads of raw materials
- Dealing with labor unions
- Getting involved in big tax problems

And how could she do this? Rose found her answer in the monthly newsletter *International Wealth Success.*
And her answer was:

Import finished products for low-overhead high-profit sales in any field

Using the book *Worldwide Riches Opportunities: 2500 Great Leads for Making Your Fortune in Overseas Trade Without Leaving Home,* she found a number of overseas toy exporters willing to send her free samples of their products. Since it was late in the season, Rose took six powerful steps to build her wealth fast. She:

(1) *Called* the overseas exporters on the telephone and arranged for samples to be air mailed to her
(2) Contacted department stores and toy wholesalers and showed them her samples

(3) Took orders for the toys
(4) Ordered by telephone the toys she needed from the overseas dealers on a 180-day payment plan
(5) Had the toys delivered to her customers by air freight
(6) Billed her customers on a 30-day payment plan

In her first season Rose billed $137,000 in toy sales after investing only $312 for telephone calls, stationery, billheads, and postage. Her profit on these sales was $52,320! Today Rose is a toy millionairess even though she has invested less than $1,000 of her own money in her business!

Get With the Money

Manny C. wanted to deal in raw land—i.e., land which is unimproved. This means, usually, that the land is without

- Sidewalks
- Street lights
- Curbs
- Street paving
- Water supply
- Sewers

Manny thought about his raw-land ambitions every night before he went to sleep. During these thought sessions Manny planned how he would:

- Find profitable raw land
- Finance land purchases
- Improve parts of the land
- Offer land for sale
- Profit from his sales

Whenever he had a chance during the day or evening, Manny read books on real-estate investments. A number of these books are listed at the end of this chapter.

One night, while thinking about the possibilities of raw-land deals, Manny put his psychic money powers to work with great success. This is how Manny turned his psychic powers into money.

Lying in the darkness of his bedroom, Manny "saw," in the

form of a large map, the land he'd been considering as a potential purchase. Around the land Manny also "saw" the towns and cities. Streets and highways stood out in sharp relief on the map.

As Manny watched the map he "saw" parts of the nearby towns and cities expand to the area where he planned to purchase raw land. The movement was so clear and precise that Manny knew exactly *where* to purchase raw land to profit from the natural expansion of nearby towns and cities.

But as Manny watched he realized that he didn't have the answer to one question—i.e.: How *fast* do towns and cities expand to take over raw land? A clock started to tick at high speed in his mind and in a moment Manny had the answer:

> Expanding towns and cities move into raw-land areas at the rate of one mile per year.

Manny didn't realize it at the time but he had actually rediscovered a well-proven principle of real estate, namely:

> Buy raw land five miles outside of town and sell at a big profit five years later.

Borrow Your Way to a Great Fortune

Manny subscribed to *International Wealth Success* and automatically became a member of their Business Borrowers Club, making him eligible to borrow:

- $1,000 to $500,000
- At competitive interest rates
- With *no* extra charges
- For one month to seven years
- In complete privacy
- With a balloon repayment plan—i.e., pay interest only once a year; pay the principal as the final payment—say in the 84th month with a 7-year loan

Manny obtained a $75,000 business loan and invested in raw land:

- One mile from town

- Two miles from town
- Three miles from town
- Four miles from town

During the next several years he sold off portions of his raw land about once a year, at an excellent profit each time. Then he took some of the profit on each deal and reinvested it in more raw land. Today Manny is a real-estate millionaire, all because he used his psychic money powers!

Practice, Practice, Practice

Since I try to be the best friend every one of my readers ever had, I get to meet thousands of new people every year. And, of course, my own business activities, which range from acquisition advice to zoology book publishing, bring me into contact with thousands of other people.

And one fact often astounds me about these people. This fact is:

> People put off until tomorrow what they could do today, even though doing it now costs them nothing and prepares them for tomorrow.

"I'll practice my psychic money powers when I need them," many of these people tell me.

"Baloney!" I reply. "Do it now—practice *now*—so you're ready when the time comes."

And how can you practice? That's easy. Just:

- Try to "see" the outcome of national and international events
- Analyze business situations you encounter and predict their outcomes
- Apply your psychic powers to personal situations

Not only should you practice; you should also keep a score of your results. Here's one scoring form that many wealth-builders find useful for keeping track of their psychic money power activities.

PSYCHIC MONEY POWER RESULTS

Month of _____ , 19__

	Situation Analyzed	My Prediction of Outcome	Actual Outcome of Situation
1.	_____	_____	_____
2.	_____	_____	_____
3.	_____	_____	_____
4.	_____	_____	_____
5.	_____	_____	_____
6.	_____	_____	_____

Sometimes you won't be able to obtain a definite outcome to a situation each month. That's no problem—just keep your record on file and fill it out when you can determine the actual outcome. Use your Psychic Money Power Results form for six months while you practice your skills and you'll:

- Improve your psychic money powers
- Become more confident
- Be a better businessman
- Soon be on your way to your first million dollars

Listen to a voice of experience—I know whereof I speak! Practice never hurt anyone. And I guarantee that it will not hurt you—particularly in the field of psychic money power!

Know the Power of Psychic Forces

Sid Z. heard of a free government bulletin giving plans for a device useful in oil fields. He sent for the bulletin. When it arrived he spent hours studying the plans. Besides gaining an understanding of the device, Sid learned that he could build and sell it, if he wanted to.

That night Sid's psychic money powers went to work and he could see hundreds of oil rigs successfully using the device, which he was already calling "his." The next day Sid borrowed $4,000 to build his device. Soon he had a number of the devices sold and operating in various oil fields. With money rolling in from the sale of his device, Sid decided to diversify. Quickly expanding his interests using borrowed money, Sid's business activities soon included:

- Oil fields
- Shipping companies
- Truck manufacture
- Banks
- Aerospace equipment
- Food processing
- Radio and television stations
- Baseball and football teams
- Overseas investments
- Air freight operations

Every business activity Sid took on is a winner. Why? "Because," he says, "I early recognized and resolved to use, the enormous forces generated by psychic money power. When you use these forces you multiply your business strength. I've seen skinny little guys develop the business power and brains of more than 100 men. How? By proper development and use of their psychic business and money powers."

You can do the same, if you will spend the time and energy to build your psychic money powers to their strongest. To get the most mileage from *your* psychic powers:

(1) Resolve, here and now, that you *will* develop your psychic powers to their strongest.
(2) Use your psychic powers whenever possible—practice makes perfect.
(3) Look for positive results—expect the best in life and you'll get it.
(4) Expect the unusual but don't be disappointed if your psychic experiences are normal without featuring way-out incidents.

Seek the Magic in Psychic Money Powers

Some businessmen tell me of their way-out experiences with psychic money powers. Many say "These psychic powers are

truly magic when it comes to making *big* money. Once I understood how to use my psychic powers my income zoomed so fast
that it rocketed out of sight."

The same thing happened to me, personally. For years I
worked hard at a number of activities—writing, mail order,
import-export, real estate, etc. But my income was only modest.
Then one day I sensed the magic of psychic money power and
within a few months my:

- Royalities zoomed upwards
- Mail order income doubled
- Import-export income quadrupled
- Real estate profits shot up

Soon the income taxes on my income were larger than the
total income I earned a year earlier. Today my income is so large
that I truly don't know what to do with 75% of the money I earn!
After all, how many Cadillacs can you drive at one time, how
many boats can you pilot out through the inlet on a bright, sunny
morning?

So I keep myself busy and in touch with a variety of businesses by lending part of my profits to my clients for business use.
This practice has made me thousands of friends and hundreds of
thousands of additional dollars. As I tell people "I have the ideal
life—riches in friends, fun, feelings, and finances!"

Yes, there is magic in psychic money power. And I'm not
talking about a phony kind of magic that people use to mislead
others. Instead, I'm talking about the kind of magic that:

- Builds strong motivation
- Puts together a success formula for you
- Blends all your drives into one
- Increases your popularity
- Gives you power over people

If that's the kind of magic you want in *your* life, then psychic
money power is worth a try.

Psychic Money Power Works Everywhere

Will T. wanted to go into the mail-order business but he had only $80 to invest to start his business. One ad in a large U.S. magazine would cost more than $80. So Will decided to:

* Seek low-cost advertising outlets
* Develop special products for these outlets
* Build each customer from a large first sale to larger future sales

Looking around, Will discovered that some of the lowest cost advertising outlets in the world are magazines in Western Europe, Japan, and South America. Comparing the rates of overseas magazines with U.S. magazines, Will found that it would cost him about half as much overseas to advertise his products. So he decided "to go foreign" with his mail order ads.

Pick Your Product Using Psychic Powers

Will was interested in music, films, and recordings of all kinds. He decided to try to make these interests pay off in mail order. Checking with various overseas countries, Will quickly found that British music buffs love American l.p. records and tapes. But these products are extremely difficult to obtain in England. So Will decided to try to sell American l.p. records and tapes through mail order in Britain.

He took a small ad in the classified column of a major British music magazine. Within days after his first ad appeared, Will began receiving money in the mail. Lucky for him, his record and tape products were:

* Easy to mail
* Low cost
* Readily manufactured
* Quickly packaged
* Cheap to reproduce if lost

It was for just these reasons that Will chose the products he

was marketing. But what he and his psychic money powers over-
looked was:

- European magazines have worldwide circulation
- People in out-of-the-way places read constantly to
  keep themselves busy
- Mail order is a way of life for people in isolated areas
- Classified columns are favorite reading for many
  music buffs

Earn Money from the Entire World

Soon Will was receiving orders from every country in the
world. The money flowed in so fast that Will had to make two
trips a day to the bank to deposit his income.

Will worked part-time on this mail-order business for a year,
his income slowly rising as each new ad appeared. But Will
sensed that something was lacking in his mail-order business. That
lack, Will gradually came to realize, was a shortage of dynamic
growth ideas for the business. He could muddle on from year
to year at a slow growth rate. But that would bring him a net income of only about $50,000 per year. This was only half of his
goal of $100,000 per year two years after starting his mail-order
business.

Put Your Psychic Money Powers to Work

Will decided that he needed help. But not from an outsider
to whom he'd have to explain the business. Instead, Will needed
help from himself—what he had to do was to rediscover himself
and his ideas. To do this Will had to put his psychic money powers
to work. After all, folks, there's no profit in having an unusual skill
unless it works for *you*!

So every night when he went to bed, Will put his psychic
money powers to work. Within days he came up with some twenty
ideas, including:

- Speculation in the foreign currencies he received
- Offer super bargains on high-priced ($100 or more)
  music libraries

- Prepare, and send to his customers, a comprehensive catalog of his products
- Accept, from countries with currency restrictions, valuable postage stamps as payment for his products
- Sell the postage stamps for cash in the U.S.
- Expand his product line to include related music items such as books, sheet music, etc.

Will expanded his business using these psychic-generated ideas. In the first year he used these ideas, Will tripled his sales and profits. In the following year he quadrupled sales and profits.

The last time I saw Will I asked him if he was thinking of changing his place of residence from the U.S. to Europe. Laughing happily, he quoted the famous Greek story of the rich man who, when asked his nationality, said "I am of the rich." Yes, reader friends, when you're rich (as I hope you will soon be) the world is your playground. And as a rich man or woman, you need no other qualifications to:

- Be welcome everywhere you go
- Have thousands of friends
- Work when and where you please
- Vacation anytime, anywhere
- Enjoy life to its fullest
- Travel, dine, and play on your business expense account
- Profit from everything you do—be it work or play
- Say goodbye forever to nasty bosses, job layoffs, pay cuts, and firings

Psychic Money Power Really Pays Off

If I haven't convinced you by now of the enormous forces generated by psychic money power, then I want to give you just one more thought, and that is this:

It won't cost you a dime to try psychic money power. So why not give it a spin today, tomorrow, and the next day? The results could astound you!

You have it within your power—at this very instant—to be

fabulously wealthy, if you use your psychic money power. Why not try? You have nothing to lose but an enormous fortune!

For a more detailed coverage of psychic power and its many uses, read a copy of Schwartz—*The Magic of Psychic Power,* Parker Publishing Co., Inc. This excellent book will show you many techniques for putting psychic power to work in your daily life.

USEFUL BOOKS ON PSYCHIC POWER

Archer—*Exploring the Psychic World,* Morrow
Bendit—*Psychic Sense,* Theosophical Publications
Brown—*The Power of Psychic Awareness,* Parker Pub. Co.
Chase—*You Can Through Psychic Power,* Grosset
Dubin—*Telecult Power,* Parker Pub. Co.
Edmunds—*Miracles of the Mind,* Thomas
Holzer—*ESP and You,* Hawthorn
Karagulla—*Breakthrough to Creativity,* DeVorss
Rhine—*New World of the Mind,* Sloane
Young—*Secrets of Personal Psychic Power,* Parker Pub. Co.

USEFUL BOOKS ON REAL ESTATE

To complete this chapter, here are a number of useful and worthwhile books on real estate which you might want to read. Apply the technique of psychic money power in real-estate deals and watch your wealth zoom!

Barr—*Miracle Real Estate Guide,* Prentice-Hall
Barrow—*Making Big Money in Real Estate,* Prentice-Hall
Berman—*How to Reap Profits in Local Real Estate Syndicates,* Prentice-Hall
Bohon—*Complete Guide to Profitable Real Estate Leasing,* Prentice-Hall
Bockl—*How to Use Leverage to Make Money in Local Real Estate,* Prentice-Hall
DeBenedictis—*10 Ways to Make a Killing in Real Estate on a Shoestring Investment,* Simon & Schuster

ERC Editorial Staff—*Today's Great Opportunities for Getting Rich in Real Estate,* Prentice-Hall

Friedman—*Handbook of Real Estate Forms,* Prentice-Hall

Gardiner—*How I Sold a Million Dollars of Real Estate in One Year,* Prentice-Hall

Gross—*Illustrated Encyclopedia Dictionary of Real Estate Terms,* Prentice-Hall

Kent—*How to Get Rich in Real Estate,* Prentice-Hall

Maisel—*Financing Real Estate,* McGraw-Hill

Nickerson—*How I Turned $1,000 into $3 Million in Real Estate in My Spare Time,* Simon & Schuster

P-H Editorial Staff—*Prentice-Hall Treasury of Money-Making: Real Estate Ideas and Practices,* Prentice-Hall

Steinberg—*Mortgage Your Way to Wealth,* Parker Pub. Co.

Stone—*How to Operate a Real Estate Trade-In Program,* Prentice-Hall

thirteen

Using Psycho-Cybernetics to Control Your Wealth

Whether we realize it or not, most of us carry two mental pictures of ourselves at all times. These pictures are:

(1) What you *think* you look like, physically
(2) What you *think* of yourself as a person (this is your *self-image*)

We can alter our physical appearance somewhat by changing the type and style of clothes we wear, by changing our body by plastic surgery, and so on. But changing what we *think* of ourselves as persons isn't as easy. Psycho-cybernetics was developed to help us change our self-image from negative to positive, and thereby improve our state in life.

Know the Basics of Psycho-Cybernetics

Dr. Maxwell Maltz, a plastic surgeon, developed psycho-cybernetics after studying the *mental* results of many of his *physical* operations. An interesting and important finding he made was:

When people thought their appearance was improved by plastic surgery, they began leading much more productive lives, even though their appearance was unchanged.

This and many similar findings proved to Dr. Maltz that:

> What we think of ourself (our self-image) is often the most important factor in our lives.

My experience in the field of fortune building verifies the Maltz findings. What my experience, and that of thousands of other wealth-builders shows, is that:

* Think *rich* and *become* rich
* Act and think *poor;* stay poor
* Act rich; grow rich
* Be positive; act positive; make progress

Think Big—Win Big

You can't win big stakes in this life if you think small. The prize goes to the man who can look beyond $200 per week to $2,000 per week to $20,000 per week.

In all my business dealings and travels I constantly note that those who think well of themselves and others usually reach great wealth. What many of these successful people intuitively sense is that thinking well of themselves and their abilities puts money in their pockets!

But not everyone has a positive self-image. Many beginning wealth-builders, I find:

* Are uncertain, insecure
* Have a negative self-image
* Think they're "bad"
* Carry many guilt feelings from the past
* Worry too much about unimportant matters.

Because so many beginning wealth-builders have these feelings I try, on our first meeting, to restore their confidence in themselves. Often, this is all they need—simply a clearer definition of their self-image.

Dr. Maltz has written a number of helpful books on psycho-cybernetics. These books are listed at the end of this chapter. If you haven't yet read a book on psycho-cybernetics, I suggest that you do so. You may be able to change your whole life by reading one of Dr. Maltz' books. In this book we will concentrate on the income and wealth aspects of psycho-cybernetics. Dr. Maltz' books deal with many other aspects that may interest you.

Plan Your Way to Riches

Some people in this life have to complicate everything. Go out to lunch with a *complicator type* and it will take him half an hour just to choose a place to eat.

Simplifiers, by contrast, go directly to the target, without wasting time or energy. In all my travels around the world I've yet to see one complicator who hit it big, but I've met thousands of simplifiers who have money "running out of their ears." This success of the simplifiers usually irritates the complicators to the point where they lose lots of sleep.

Now a simplifier does just what has to be done, and nothing more. You can use the simplification technique to *think yourself rich!* But before I tell you how you can think yourself rich, let me tell you about a few people who did this for themselves.

Use the Psycho-Cybernetics Way to Wealth

Three men decided to "get rich" within a year. By "getting rich," each man meant accumulating $100,000 profit in one year in a business of his own. But they agreed to approach their problem in three different ways:

- One man would *work* at *his* business for twelve months
- One man would *think* for six months about working at *his* business
- One man would do *nothing* about *his* business for six months
- After six months the two men who didn't work would start working

The men did as planned. At the end of the second six months here's how the three businessmen stood with respect to their goal:

No. 1 (worked all year): $101,000 profit
No. 2 (thought 6 months,
         worked 6 months): $ 98,000 profit
No. 3 (worked 6 months): $ 17,000 profit

The actual situation shows how effective psycho-cybernetics can be. Thus, the man who just *thought about* his business for 6 months was able to earn nearly exactly the same amount as the man who had worked *all* year at his own business.

Develop a Positive Self-Image

"All the world loves a winner"—what this saying attempts to summarize is the worldwide love of and affection for a winner who:

* Has a *positive* self-image
* Develops his skills to the utmost
* Succeeds where others fail
* Knows himself and his skills

When you have a positive self-image, you:

(1) Believe in yourself
(2) Know what you can do
(3) Transmit your positiveness to others
(4) Earn big money fast

Become an Instant Millionaire

Some people like a slow, plodding way to wealth. But most people, I find, prefer instant wealth. Why? Because:

The longer a person does without an object he seeks,
the more impatient he becomes to possess it.

Claire P. wanted to become an instant millionairess. When I talked to her, I asked her what her major interest in life was. "I really have two, Ty," she replied. "My first major interest is real estate, and my second is oil wells."

"Great," I said. "Either one lends itself to making you an instant millionaire."

"How can that be done?" she asked, puzzled.

Here's the plan I outlined for her. The same plan, in much greater detail, and full of specific instructions with step-by-step guides and forms, is marketed by IWS, Inc., P.O. Box 186, Merrick, N.Y. 11566, for $99.50. If you want to become an instant millionaire, you might like to obtain their multi-volume program for yourself.

The plan I outlined for Claire was:

THE INSTANT-MILLIONAIRE PLAN

1. Decide how much money you need for your investment (in Claire's case her first investment was real estate).
2. Form a *limited partnership* to operate your business (ideal for real estate).
3. Register the limited partnership in your state (have your lawyer do this for you).
4. Sell enough *shares* or *units* in the partnership to generate the cash you seek (you can obtain hundreds to millions of dollars).
5. Begin your business (work hard).
6. Pay yourself a suitable salary for the work you do (be fair in the rewards you pay yourself).

Claire P. decided to buy land which was ready for development into shopping centers or residential areas. Studying this type of land near her home, Claire found that she would need $5,000,000 to get started. Forming a limited partnership in her state, Claire soon sold 1,000 shares in the partnership at $5,000 each. Thus, within just a few months she became an instant millionairess! "And it was very easy to do," Claire says, "because I had a favorable self-image!"

Get All the Facts

"Ty," you say with growing interest, "I want to know more about this instant millionaire bit. Will you answer a few questions?"

"Sure, anything you want to know. Ask and you shall receive."

Q. Do I need previous experience in a business to form a limited partnership for the business?

A. No; many limited partnerships are formed to engage in a business in which the partnership has yet to earn a penny.

Q. What is a limited partnership?

A. A limited partnership is one in which the liability of the *limited* (or *special partners* as they are also called) is restricted to the amount of money the partner has put into the venture. Thus, if a limited partnership share is sold for $5,000, this amount is the maximum liability for which the limited or special partner can be held.

Q. Can limited partnerships go public?

A. Yes, a limited partnership can sell units, shares, or participations to the general public. When a limited partnership goes public there are a number of advantages, including:

* Acquisition of a large sum of money
* No repayments of the money required
* Special or limited partners have no vote in company operation
* Major tax advantages to each limited partner

Q. Should I have a lawyer help me form a limited partnership?

A. Positively yes! Don't try to be your own legal eagle—you'll live to regret it. And if you plan to go public, you *must* have a lawyer for the formation of your limited partnership.

Q. What other advantages does the limited partnership have?

A. Many, including:

* Possibility of quick formation
* Easier registration requirements
* Money is obtained in large amounts
* Control of company is not given up

Q. Why do people buy into limited partnerships?

A. Because this type of investment allows them to go into a specific business by just investing money—they don't have to work at the business; the general partners usually do that. Also, there are specific income-tax advantages for high income persons.

Q. What are the typical share or participation prices in limited partnerships?

A. Typical share or participation prices range from $1,000 to $10,000 per share, with $5,000 being a popular price. The revenue to the partnership that could be produced by the sale of 1,000 units or shares at various prices is given below.

Number of Shares Sold	Price per Share	Total Share Revenue to the Partnership
1,000	$1,000	$1,000,000
1,000	2,000	2,000,000
1,000	3,000	3,000,000
1,000	4,000	4,000,000
1,000	5,000	5,000,000
1,000	6,000	6,000,000
1,000	8,000	8,000,000
1,000	10,000	10,000,000

This listing clearly shows that a sale of only 1,000 shares can bring you an income of $1,000,000 to $10,000,000, depending on the price you charge per share.

Q. How does becoming an instant millionaire relate to psycho-cybernetics?

A. Here's how. With a favorable self-image you can, more readily:

- Charge a higher price per share
- Sell more shares yourself
- Attract more desirable people to your company

Keep Setting Goals for Yourself

Dr. Maltz, in explaining how he developed the concept of psycho-cybernetics, places great emphasis on setting goals in life and striving to achieve these goals. In my dealings with thousands of Beginning Wealth-Builders (BWBs), I find that many of them don't:

- Have specific money goals
- Realize the importance of time
- Keep striving after their goals

You need money goals, I need money goals, large corporations need money goals—everyone everywhere needs money goals! And to be effective your money goals must:

- State the amount you seek
- Specify the date by which you will obtain the money
- Tell how you'll earn the money

Without these three hows, i.e., *how much, how soon,* and just plain *how,* your money goal will not be clear, defined, and numbered. To hit the big money, all of us need specific, measurable goals. Knowing how much we seek and the time limit we've imposed on our goal, we can easily measure *actual* progress and compare this with our *planned* progress. When we fall behind schedule, we *take action* to bring our actual results into line with our planned results.

A Big-Money Goal and Your Self-Image

Now let me reveal a key money secret which I've known for years and have seen work thousands of times. This cash-laden secret is:

The greater your self-image, the easier it is for you to choose a suitable money goal, and the more likely it is that you will achieve your money goal!

Of the thousands of wealth-builders I've known and worked with, not one having a favorable self-image failed to hit the *big* money. True, some took a little longer than others to reach the top. But they all eventually made a bundle through honest, hard work.

Let me give you a few examples.

ACTUAL RECORDS OF BEGINNING WEALTH-BUILDERS

Business Chosen by BWB	Money Goal (i.e., profit)	Time to Reach Goal	Remarks
"New" antiques sales	$250,000	18 months	Started on OPM
Real-estate speculation	$1,000,000	56 months	Still growing
Mail-order drop shipping	$125,000	11 months	Sold at a big gain
Spare-time export-import	$200,000	14 months	Now a full-time business
Music and show recording	$ 75,000	5 months	Sold to brother
Financial broker	$800,000	42 months	Still growing

There are hundreds of other beginning wealth-builders I could list here. But their actual records are much like those shown above. The only fact you would get from the extra listing is a verification that:

Improving your self-image raises your chances of success enormously, while making you happier and more interesting to others.

Seek the Unusual Everywhere

My business trips take me all over the world. While I'm on these trips I try to see as much of each country and city as I can. I do this by taking the available bus and boat tours. Then, at night, after dinner, I stroll the streets while enjoying my evening cigar. It is during these evening strolls that I often meet unusual people in way-out businesses.

While I don't recommend evening strolls through strange cities as a way to get rich, I do suggest that you:

- Seek unusual business ideas everywhere
- Spend more time listening than talking
- Try to learn something from every person you meet
- Avoid wasting time on what you already know
- Get others to talk about themselves while you listen
- Ask questions—seek information
- Make notes about what you learn
- Review your notes frequently

Finding the unusual helps you improve your self-image in many ways, including:

(1) Setting you apart from others

(2) Making you a wanted guest everywhere

(3) Giving you a feeling of truly being "different"

(4) Improving your poise

Let's see how seeking the unusual worked out for one fortune builder.

Turn Your Self-Image into Cash

Ronald C. always sought the unusual wherever he went. And coincidentally, Ronald's main interest in life was antiques. Not only did Ronald want to collect antiques, he also wanted to sell them.

While on a vacation trip to the far West, Ronald came across a number of 1890 barber poles and barber chairs. Something told him that these items, while not truly antiques, might be worth money in the Eastern antique market. So Ronald bought six barber poles and six chairs and had them shipped east to his home.

As soon as he arrived home, Ronald called on several local antique dealers. Talking to them, he was delighted to learn that he could sell the poles for four times his cost, and the chairs for six times his cost. The dealers called his items "junk" antiques.

Studying the junk antique market, Ronald soon came up with a list of typical going prices for various items, some of which are listed below. Should you be interested in junk antiques and take the time to check these prices, you'll probably find that the actual prices you're quoted are higher. Why? Because as time passes, the prices of antiques are constantly rising.

Why do I recommend that you consider junk antiques, if this field interests you? Because junk antiques:

- Are easy to find
- Don't cost much
- Show a good profit
- Can earn you a fortune
- Seldom cause problems

Now here are typical junk antique prices existing at the time of the writing of this book.

TYPICAL JUNK ANTIQUE PRICES

Item	Selling Price
1930 telephone signs	$8.00
1920 vintage soda bottles	12.50
1900 vintage gum-ball machine	200.00
1930 "cathedral-type" radio	75.00
Kewpie dolls, 1930	25.00
Wooden ice box, good condition	150.00
Colored-glass telephone-pole insulators, each	12.00
Porcelain chamber pots	30.00
Early American bath tubs	100.00
Dental chairs	100.00
Old Coca-Cola bottles	10.00
Buck Rogers gun	40.00
Barber pole	150.00
Cigarette and cigar posters	50.00 to 150.00
Coca-Cola clocks	150.00

Hundreds and hundreds of other items could be added to this list. That's exactly what Ronald did to organize his antique Search, Buy, and Sell business, which you'll hear about in the next paragraph.

Switch a Good Idea into Millions

Recognizing that he was on to something big, Ronald decided that what he needed was volume. So he listed the four steps he'd have to take to make a profit in the junk antique business:

(1) Recruit antique search-and-find personnel
(2) Search and find suitable antiques using the personnel recruited
(3) Buy the antiques at acceptable prices
(4) Sell the purchased antiques at profitable prices

To recruit his Search and Find personnel, Ronald placed low-cost ads in small-town newspapers. He was flooded with responses from women throughout the country who love to:

- Search and find antiques
- Work part-time
- Earn some extra money
- Make buying decisions
- Spend someone else's money

Sell for More Than You Pay

Once he had his buyers lined up, Ronald wrote to hundreds of antique stores, telling them about his Search and Find capabilities. He had an immediate positive response, with many specific orders from more than half the stores. "So I put my 'troops' into action," Ronald says with a laugh. "They turned up three-hundred and eight wanted items the first week. And do you know what my profit on those items was? A sweet two-thousand seven-hundred and twelve dollars! Today my weekly profit exceeds three-thousand dollars, every week of the year. And all because I like myself—i.e., I have a favorable self-image."

Learn from Everyone

Now I don't say that "junk" antiques are your thing. But the steps I've listed above that Ronald took apply to any business, anywhere. So if you want to convert your self-image into cash, consider using the steps shown above. At most, you won't lose anything except some time. And most BWBs have plenty of time on their hands!

Now let's see if you can learn a little from me—on strictly a friend-to-friend basis. What I'd like to have you learn will put cash in your pocket and happiness in my heart. Could anyone ask for a better deal? Certainly, I couldn't. What I want you to learn is just this:

> An improved self-image will make your life more fruit-ful and bring you greater happiness. You must work at improving your self-image, but the results will repay you every day of your life!

You Must Like Yourself

Every year, amongst the beginning wealth-builders I meet, are some who are unsuccessful and unhappy because they don't like themselves! Your first job, I tell them, is not to make a million. Instead it is to:

* Accept yourself as you are today
* Resolve to improve your self-image
* Start thinking deeply about getting rich
* Take action to improve your business skills
* Work hard; think a lot; study constantly

Psycho-cybernetics wasn't developed simply to make you rich. Instead, Dr. Maltz developed his excellent methods as aids to improving the happiness of every human being. But you can combine happiness and wealth by using psycho-cybernetics wisely. Could you ask for anything more than a happy man or woman with plenty of money in the bank? Try psycho-cybernetics and see!

Now here are some excellent books on self-image psychology and related topics. Read as many of these books, as soon as you can. You'll find that you'll soon:

* Accept yourself more readily
* Lose many fears you now have

- Obtain a new sense of direction for your life
- Set—and achieve—important goals

USEFUL BOOKS FOR BUILDING AN
IMPROVED SELF-IMAGE

Bristol—*The Magic of Believing*, Prentice-Hall
Hill—*Grow Rich with Peace of Mind*, Fawcett
Hill—*The Master-Key to Riches*, Fawcett
Hill—*Think and Grow Rich*, Fawcett
Hutschnecker—*The Will to Live*, Prentice-Hall
Maltz—*Creative Living for Today*, Trident Press
Maltz—*The Magic Power of Self-Image Psychology*, Prentice-Hall
Maltz—*Psycho-Cybernetics*, Prentice-Hall
Morgan and Webb—*Making the Most of Your Life*, Doubleday and Co.
Peterson—*New Life Begins at Forty*, Pocket Books
Schindler—*How to Live 365 Days a Year*, Prentice-Hall
Warner—*Self-Realization and Self-Defeat*, Grove Press

fourteen

How to Grow
Richer with the
Newest Mind Methods

Your mind is the greatest power plant in the world. Why? Because *your* mind can:

- Generate thousands of profitable ideas
- Find improvements for existing techniques
- Solve money problems of all kinds
- Do anything you direct it to

Since I am so convinced of these facts, I spent a year writing this book to convince you of the truthfulness and usefulness of these facts about *your* mind. Truly, friend, I have nothing to sell you except *your* success!

Think the Big-Success Way

You may not believe me when I tell you about the magic power of your mind. Fine—I respect your disbelief. But if I back up my claims with evidence that some of the biggest and most successful corporations and universities in the world believe in

217

the power of the mind, you may be more likely to believe me. And if I showed you my personal income-tax return and the tax returns of my various businesses, I'm certain you'd instantly believe. You might even shout "Show me the way to do one-tenth as well as you have!"

If you asked several experts to list the firms and schools that believe in the enormous power of the mind to solve all kinds of practical and theoretical problems, these experts would quickly list for you names such as:

General Electric Company
McDonnell-Douglas Corporation
Texas Instruments Incorporated
Massachusetts Institute of Technology
Harvard University
Arthur D. Little, Inc.

Hundreds of other firms and universities throughout the world could easily be added to this list. But the whole point is this:

Big successes everywhere—be they individuals, firms, or schools—believe in, and use, the power of the mind to solve practical business problems. And you can do the same to solve your money problems quickly and easily!

Try the Newest Approaches

In recent years many new methods for solving business problems have been developed, including:

• Brainstorming
• Horizontal think
• Group think
• Potential problem analysis
• Logic design
• Creative thinking
• Synthesis

You can use any or all of these mind methods to solve *your* money problems. Or you can develop a method of your own which may be better than any of these. Great! Write a good book or article and tell the world about your method!

Now let's take a quick look at each of these methods to see how you can use it in building *your* wealth. In the process of looking at these methods we might create your fortune!

Brainstorm Your Way to Wealth

Brainstorming is the process of thinking about problems in a free and unrestrained way. In the usual brainstorming session, several people sit around a table and call out ideas for solving a problem. A secretary writes down the various ideas on a blackboard or in a notebook.

Later, after the session is over, one or more people sit down and carefully analyze the ideas that were generated in the brainstorming session. During the actual brainstorming, you:

- Free associate as much as possible
- Don't censor any ideas
- Have one idea trigger another
- Keep coming up with new ideas until fatigue sets in
- Evaluate ideas *after* the session, not during the session

"But," you say, "I don't want several people in on my money ideas. They might take them and use the ideas before I can."

"Fine," I say. "Brainstorm by yourself." Here's how.

Hold Private Brainstorming Sessions

Go to a quiet room where you won't be disturbed. Using a portable tape recorder, or a large notebook, either call out or jot down money ideas as they come to you. I find that calling out ideas is best, no matter how you record them. Why? Because one idea that is called out seems to more readily trigger a second idea, and a third, and so on. Jotting ideas down in silence doesn't seem to work as well for most people as calling them out.

Continue calling out ideas and writing them down until you feel tired. Then stop and do something else for a day or so. Go back to your notebook list of ideas from your brainstorming session when you have an hour or more available to spend on them.

Study each idea carefully. Discard those ideas that seem

too wild to ever work. List the ideas which seem to have real potential.

Next, study your list of ideas having potential. Try to see how you can get started with one of these ideas so that it begins earning money for you fast. Let's see how a Beginning Wealth-Builder (BWB) actually did this.

Good Ideas Make Money

Johnnie K. was fifty—broke, discouraged, and ready to give up altogether. Yet he kept telling himself "Just one more try and I may make it." Without knowing it Johnnie was a believer in the "Hicks Law on How to Get Rich" which is:

(1) You *must* find a way to build your wealth
(2) *Build* on your past experience
(3) *Never* cease trying
(4) Use every *honest* means you can
(5) Push on to *win* every time

Johnnie heard about brainstorming and decided that it might be an answer to his money problems. So he brainstormed the problem of quickly finding a way to great wealth. This is what Johnnie found:

Brainstorming Session No.	*Findings*
1	Seeking a way to wealth isn't easy
2	He needed the simplest, fastest possible way to wealth
3	Big investments, long delays were not for him
4	He'd like to sell expensive items to rich buyers
5	Selling a unique product to large companies could make him rich
6	He'd develop, and sell, a printed product to large companies

True to his plan, Johnnie developed several printed products, including:

- Work planning forms
- Time estimating calculators
- Lists of useful data

In developing these products, Johnnie used his past experience in industry (Step 2 above) as a guide to products that would sell well.

Never Stop Trying

Equipped with several shiny new samples of his products (prepared free of charge by a printer), Johnnie visited local firms and tried to sell as many items of his products as he could. He worked steadily for two weeks and his score was exactly zero.

Pondering his failures on Friday evening of the second week, Johnnie tried to determine what was wrong. This session showed him that:

- People didn't have time to listen to his sales pitch
- He seldom could get to see the right man—i.e., the one who both understood his product and had the authority to buy his products
- He needed more time than people had to get his sales pitch for his products across

Figuring that he had to either make his fortune with these products or give up, Johnnie decided to brainstorm his sales technique. "I'll never stop trying," he promised himself.

His brainstorming quickly showed Johnnie that:

(a) He needed a better way to give his sales pitch
(b) His better method must allow more time for presenting his story
(c) The better method must be directed at the man or woman who understood and had the authority to purchase the products

The more Johnnie analyzed his problem the clearer it became that he needed a unique sales method. Then, one day while reading the newsletter *International Wealth Success* he found his answer. A short item asked: "Have you ever mined the golden riches of *industrial mail order?* If you haven't, you should take a look at this:

* Rich, payment-ready market
* Easy-to-reach market
* Constantly growing market

Here's how you can be one of the few smart-money people who cash in every day on this, the richest market in the world." The article went on to give specific, step-by-step procedures.

As soon as he read these words Johnnie knew he had the answer he needed. Within a few hours he roughed out his mail order plans. In a week his first mailing was on its way. Less than a week later Johnnie received his first order, accompanied by an insured check. Today Johnnie is averaging a profit of over $10,000 per month without ever leaving his home except to go to the post office to drop off or pick up his mail! (He banks his checks by mail.)

Try the Horizontal Think

Almost all of us think in a "vertical" manner, i.e., from a problem to its cause, to its solution, or A to B to C. In the *horizontal think* we "cut across" our problems exploring the problem itself in greater detail, searching out the cause so we clearly understand every aspect of it, and choosing the best solution we can. What the horizontal think does for you is to give you:

* New views of your problems
* Better ways to earn a fast fortune
* Quick answers to your questions

Why spend thirty years to make a million when anyone can make a million dollars in three years, or less?

Put Your Brain to Work

Charlie K. used the horizontal think to build his fortune in antique autos. Always interested in old autos, Charlie found an ancient 1932 Cadillac V-16 in a local farm dump. The farmer *paid* Charlie $5 to haul the rusty wreck away.

Charlie spent four months of his spare time overhauling and restoring the Cadillac. During this time he invested $612 in spare and replacement parts.

When the car was restored Charlie drove it to a vintage-car meet. He hoped to show the car to a few interested people who, he thought, might offer him $1,000 for it. To Charlie's amazement his car was the center of attraction at the meet, even though he didn't enter it in any competitions. And Charlie nearly fainted when one excited buyer offered him $36,000 for the car! That's when Charlie decided to apply the horizontal think.

Build on Your Skills

The usual mechanic, when faced with Charlie's sudden wealth would:

* Run out to find more old cars
* Hire people to fix the cars
* Display his cars at large exhibits at meets

Charlie analyzed each of these actions and decided his best course of action was to:

* Learn which cars were most wanted
* Develop a systematic search procedure for the most wanted cars
* Build a group of spare-time mechanics to work on the cars

As you can see, Charlie approached his problem from the side—the horizontal think. Today he earns over $200,000 a year *profit* restoring antique cars. And in case you're a classic car buff, Charlie told me that typical going prices for restored antique cars at the time of the writing of this book were:

Make and Year	*Price of Restored Car*
1929 Cadillac	$4,000
1936 Pierce Arrow	6,000
1932 Cadillac V-16	40,000
1932 Packard V-12	30,000

Maybe You Need Group Think

If you aren't rich yet, perhaps you need the *group think*. What's this? It's a little like brainstorming—you just get a group of interested people to think of ways to solve your problem of making a fortune.

Does group think work? Sometimes it does, and sometimes it doesn't. If people in the group are really interested in *your* problem, you may get it solved. But if the group is only mildly interested in you and your problem, the results you obtain can be less than great.

My version of the group think uses only two people—yourself and one other interested and informed expert. Using this approach with hundreds of clients, I've been able to put them on the road to wealth. But, of course, my time must be paid for—and it isn't cheap.

Where you'd prefer a do-it-yourself approach to the group think, I believe you'll be interested in the IWS *Instant Millionaire Program* listed at the end of this book. If you obtain this program, its first section, called "You *Must* Find a Way" will show you how to apply both the horizontal think and the group think to finding *your* particular road to riches.

Cure Problems Before They Occur

Many BWBs get into trouble early in their search for wealth because they don't think ahead to try to see the problems they may meet. This is unfortunate because many wasted hours could be saved and turned into *big* profits.

The newest technique for reducing business troubles is called *Potential Problem Analysis* (PPA). To use PPA, you look ahead and:

(1) Decide what problems *might* occur
(2) Rate the *seriousness* of each potential problem
(3) Choose the *corrective action* you'll take *if* the problem occurs

(4) Set up some form of *information feedback* to tell you if any problems are developing

Make Dry Runs

PPA is great—even if you never have a problem. Why? Because PPA forces you to face problems that *can* occur in the business world. This act of thinking ahead:

- Helps you see money situations in realistic terms
- Shows what solutions are possible
- Gives you dry-run experience at little cost

So try PPA today even though you aren't yet in business. To dry-run a PPA session just:

(1) Assume you're in a specific business
(2) Visualize taking orders, paying bills, etc.
(3) List the problems you might meet
(4) Select, and list your solutions of these problems
(5) Talk to people in the business to determine if your solutions would work

Practice Now—Profit Sooner

You can accomplish anything you believe you can. The world is yours for the asking. All you have to do is get out of that easy chair and start asking!

So, too, with PPA. All you need do is to start anticipating and solving problems in your head. Within days you'll become more efficient, more capable, and readier to be richer! And it won't cost you a dime. So start today and watch the golden results of mind-magic at work!

Put Logic to Work for Yourself

We all need the "good serving men" mentioned by Kipling. But today's best serving man is *logic design and technique* that came to the business world along with the computer.

Now don't let the words logic design throw you. All they mean is that you must be ready for what will probably (i.e., logically) happen in the business you choose to enter.

Watch Logic at Work

A good friend, Milton R., owns a string of taverns which give him a net income of $210,000 a year. Yet three years ago, when Milt was just starting with his first tavern, he almost kicked the entire business. Why? Because he had neglected logic design. Here's what happened.

Milt bought the first tavern using 100% financing obtained from IWS. For the first four months everything went beautifully. The money poured in as the refreshments poured across the mahogany. Milt had purchased his first tavern on the basis of an expected income of $1,800 per week. To his delight, his income averaged $2,200 per week. He was really riding high.

Then disaster (Milt thought) struck. Several customers became overenthused about a football game on TV one night and started throwing refreshment glasses at each other. A few punches were exchanged without much harm being done. Then someone called the police, and Milt. He arrived amidst the scream of sirens and the flashing of red police lights. Milt was shattered because he thought his business was ruined. The police just laughed; and the customers went back to their football game on TV and their new glasses on the mahogany.

Next day Milt called his lawyer, thoroughly discouraged. "I'll have to close the place," Milt moaned. Then Milt told the lawyer what had happened the previous evening.

When Milt finished the lawyer laughed long and hard. "Milt," he said mirthfully, "*it just figures.*"

"What do you mean 'it just figures'?" Milt asked, annoyed.

"Just this," the lawyer said. "The *logic* of the situation says that people who own taverns will have customers who will fight now and then in their place of business. Thus, it figures. See what I mean?"

Milt saw—and heaved a sigh of relief. "Just like in the trucking business I'd have flat tires now and then," Milt laughed.

"Exactly," said his lawyer. "It just figures!"
So what can you learn from this? Just this.

Figure the logic of your business in advance and little
can happen to you or your business for which you won't
be prepared.

Logic design may seem complicated but it really isn't. And
it doesn't cost you a dime!

Increase Your Creativity

Creative ideas can win you big profits, be the ideas simple
or complex. And your creative ideas needn't be confined to a new
product such as a better mousetrap that makes you a millionaire.
You can be highly creative about the simplest aspects of your
business. Sometimes the smallest shortcuts, kinks, or methods you
think up earn you the biggest return.

Your mind is a powerhouse full of wonderful ideas. All you
need do is pay a little more attention to this great tool which you
carry around with yourself inside your head twenty-four hours
a day!

To develop your creative powers (and we all have them),
take these six lucky, money-laden steps:

(1) Recognize—here and now—that *you* can be more creative
(2) Resolve—starting this very moment—that you *will* be
more creative
(3) Approach each of your problems with enthusiasm, confidence, and an open mind
(4) Make lists of creative solutions for each problem you
have
(5) Apply brainstorming, the horizontal think, the group
think, etc., to solve your problems
(6) Seek the creative way in every thing you do

Creativity Really Pays Off

I could, if we had the space, tell you about hundreds of people who've hit the big money with just one creative idea. Here are just a few that come to mind while I'm writing.

* An author made more than $100,000 in mail order in one year from a creative idea he got while sitting on a train.
* An inventor made three million dollars in one year from a gadget he thought of while taking a shower.
* A railroad conductor made two million dollars from an idea he had while walking to work one day.

Make All Your Ideas Good Ones

To make *all* your ideas *good* ideas, use these six steps:

(1) Think big—don't bother with small, time-consuming deals.
(2) Be practical—don't try to take on a business that is too big for you.
(3) Spend much of your think time on ways to get the business capital you need.
(4) Be certain that the deals you consider will throw off enough cash to put you in the chips.
(5) Seek fast, honest riches as opposed to slow, long-term plodding work.
(6) Work hard at reaching your goal.

Weed Out the Bad Ideas

Here are a few bad ideas (at least in my opinion) which were recently proposed to me:

* A man wanted to borrow $750,000 to buy 4,000 acres of land to farm himself. (Faults: Too big a loan; too much work for one man.)

- A lady wanted to rent a large building in which she could give parties for pay for local children. (Faults: Not enough income potential to pay the high rent; long-range potential too small.)

- A man wanted to borrow $500,000 to buy a factory. But he had no organization of any kind behind him. (Faults: Without a company of some sort behind you, there is little chance of borrowing large sums of money).

- A man wanted to incorporate his firm and sell stock to the public *without* using a lawyer. (Faults: You can get into all sorts of trouble when you try to save money by doing without an attorney. Save now; be sorry later!)

So learn today how to weed out the impractical, the silly, the wild. Substitute instead the practical, the profitable, and the powerful idea. You *can* be more creative—your mind has all the skills it needs. Just give them a little practice, starting right now!

Try Synthesis to Improve Your Ideas

Every fortune is built on an idea. This is true of every business in the world. That's why mind-magic is so important to you. And I'm so dedicated to making you rich that I want to show you every way possible to earn your fortune.

One of the newest ways to solve business problems is *Synthesis*, which is a problem-solving method based on the bringing together of different and unrelated elements to solve a problem. In applying Synthesis you usually put two or more minds to work on your problem. You bring together people with diverse backgrounds and experience to solve your problem, after stating it concisely so everyone can understand the problem.

To show you how this works, a group of my friends and myself recently solved a problem for a BWB. Here's how we stated his problem:

- Objective of BWB: $150,000 a year income

- Income source: Used auto business
- Items lacking: Cash for business financing; suitable going business to buy.
- Problem: How to put this man into business

We assembled a board of five people to solve this problem. Each of these people was carefully chosen so each had a unique and different background. Thus, we had a:

- Businessman (hardware store owner)
- Plumber
- Insurance executive
- Undertaker
- Toy salesman

We hoped that, using the techniques of Synthesis, we could draw on the diverse backgrounds of these people and come up with a highly creative solution to this problem. Note that we had neither used-car dealers nor car salesmen on our board.

Recognize Every Man's Worth

"How could a plumber tell you anything about the used-car business?" you ask.

"He couldn't tell us much about the used-car business," I reply. "But his ideas were bound to be different—and creative. The same is true about our other board members."

Here are the solutions we came up with, using the suggestions from our many-faceted Synthesis group:

- Find a suitable used-car business by advertising in unusual papers and magazines, by contacting big used-car lots advertising in the yellow pages, and by watching the obituaries for the demise of used-car lot owners.
- Raise the needed cash by using a compensating-balance loan.
- Advertise the lot widely once it is purchased; use radio, TV, and newspaper ads.

Today this lot shows a profit of more than $200,000 a year

for its owner. Why? Because the deal was made using good ideas as a starter, and because the owner works hard.

In another Synthesis study we advised racehorse owners and potential owners on which animals to purchase. Here's a record of the results obtained.

Animal	Purchase price	Winnings	Sale price
A	$ 5,000	$500,000	$ 700,000
B	30,000	600,000	1,750,000
C	700	850,000	Still active
D	3,500	329,000	250,000
E	2,000	712,000	1,200,000
F	1,800	422,000	Still active

Synthesis is also used by some of the largest companies in the world to solve their problems. Try this technique today on your business problems and watch your income increase.

Build Your Riches Fast

Magic mind secrets are the key to building your riches fast—starting with little or no capital. In this book I've tried to get you started on using these magic mind secrets in *your* life. Why? Because I know from my income-tax returns, and from the tax returns of the people I advise, that these magic mind secrets:

• Work for many people
• Pay off in big earnings
• Continue to work for years and years
• Help you overcome emotional slumps
• Give you daily enthusiasm

You *can* make your fortune quickly, if you use the techniques given in this and my other money books. Also, I suggest that you take a look at the other books, publications, and courses listed immediately after the end of this chapter. You will find them interesting and helpful because I have chosen them especially for *you*.

Helpful Money Books

Following are a number of useful books that will help you find sources of business capital, develop business leads, buy a business, and so on. If you have the time, I suggest that you study one or more of these books. You will find that your study will pay off in big, rich profits. For, as Aldous Huxley said: "Every man who knows how to read has it in his power to magnify himself, to multiply the ways in which he exists, to make his life full, significant, and interesting."

Business Capital Sources, $15, IWS Inc., P.O. Box 186, Merrick, N.Y. 11566. Hundreds of names and addresses of lenders—banks, finance companies, insurance companies, private firms, etc.—interested in lending up to 100 percent on many business, real-estate, and other projects. Also covers Small Business Administration loans, and going public.

Worldwide Riches Opportunities: 2500 Great Leads for Making Your Fortune in Overseas Trade Without Leaving Home, $25, IWS Inc., P.O. Box 186, Merrick, N.Y. 11566. Lists names and addresses of thousands of firms throughout the world that want to buy hundreds of thousands of different U.S. products. Also listed are hundreds of overseas firms offering salable imports, and hundreds of overseas firms wanting to be sales representatives (at no charge) for U.S. firms. Many of the firms listed will lend money or extend credit on business deals.

Acquiring and Merging Businesses, by J.H. Hennessy, Jr., $19.95, Prentice-Hall, Inc., Englewood Cliffs, N.J. 07632. Tells you how to find, screen, and acquire companies using borrowed money, treasury cash, the stock of your own company, etc. Use this guide and you'll learn where to look for acquisition candidates, how to measure the value (to you) of companies, tax advantages and disadvantages of six taxable and four non-taxable acquisition transactions, how to execute the acquisition project, etc.

Long-Term Financing, by John F. Childs, $19.95, Prentice-Hall, Inc., Englewood Cliffs, N.J. 07632. This step-by-step guide to managing your company's finances and setting its profit goals covers many topics, including: capital structure, dividend policy, financing program, types of securities, selling senior securities (i.e., bonds and preferred stock), selling common stock, investor relations, profit goals, cost of capital, and tests of good financial management. This helpful book will enable you to plan your business operations so you earn the profit you seek.

Dillavou & Howard's Principles of Business Law, 8th Edition, Robert, W. & Corley, R., $11.95, Prentice-Hall, Inc., Englewood Cliffs, N.J. 07632. Covers more than 2,400 topics in easy-to-understand business language without legal jargon. Summaries of important cases that set judicial precedents are presented. In addition, the book has a 500-term glossary listing terms ranging from abandonment to wills. This is a book that will help you avoid trouble by telling and showing you what to do before you take action.

Direct Costing Techniques for Industry, by Sam M. Woolsey, $19.95, Prentice-Hall, Inc., Englewood Cliffs, N.J. 07632. This book shows you how to use the most modern technique for planning, controlling, and building your business profits. When you use direct costing you develop more dependable data for decision making, set up more effective budgets, use labor and materials more efficiently, maximize your operating profits, and know the exact amount of cash flow each order generates in your business.

How to Build A Second-Income Fortune in Your Spare Time, by Tyler G. Hicks, $7.95, Parker Publishing Co., Inc., West Nyack, N.Y. 10994. Hundreds of useful ideas on starting and getting rich in your own business, using OPM. While you're considering this book, you should also read three others by the same author, each available from this publisher at the same price. These books are: *Smart Money Shortcuts to Becoming Rich*, and *How to Start Your Own Business on a Shoestring and Make Up to $100,000 per Year*, and *How to Borrow Your Way to a Great Fortune*.

A Complete Guide to Making a Public Stock Offering, by Elmer L. Winter, $19.95, Prentice-Hall, Inc., Englewood Cliffs, N.J. 07632. This is a step-by-step guide for going public, i.e., selling your firm's stock to the public. Using this guide, you should be able to make your stock offering quickly, efficiently, and economically. This big guide covers both Regulation A and full offerings. If you're thinking of selling stock to the public, you should have this book on hand.

Tax Guide for Buying and Selling a Business, 2nd edition, $19.95, by Stanley Hagendorf, Prentice-Hall, Inc., Englewood Cliffs, N.J. 07632. Gives over 100 examples of typical buying and selling transactions of sole proprietorships, partnerships, and corporations. Shows you how to avoid hidden tax traps that can lead to excessive or unnecessary taxes. If you're thinking of buying a business, you should have a copy of this book.

SBIC Directory and Handbook of Small Business Finance, $15, IWS, Inc., P.O. Box 186, Merrick, N.Y. 11566. Lists the names and addresses of some 400 Small Business Investment Companies. These firms lend money to small businesses, as well as buying stocks or bonds in these businesses. Loan terms range from five years to 20 years. The book also gives many useful hints on financing and operating a small or medium-sized business successfully.

Index